→ Praise for *Never Do*

"**It felt just like Rod was talking to me**, which brought lots of laugh-out-loud moments, tears to my eyes and everything in between. I couldn't wait to turn the page and read the next chapter. The only thing I didn't like was when the book came to an end. The book is inspiring and an excellent example of how life should be lived. I can't wait to see the Netflix series or movie, *Never Do Anything Just Right!*"

—**Marilyn Mitzel**, award-winning journalist

"**A wild toboggan ride through life,** from a small North Dakota town to the far ends of the world and finally, the beautiful beaches of North Carolina—proving the author picked up a little wisdom along the way. Told in Jahner's signature style, with his uniquely dry, American wit, this memoir is ***fun***.

—**Marc de Celle**, bestselling author, *How Fargo of You*

"**Highly recommended read!** What a wild ride! *Never Do Anything Just Right* is a fabulous story of a life well lived—from small town boy in North Dakota to international expatriate soaking up delicious cultures across Asia Pacific and more. I laughed, I rolled my eyes... The family love, lessons learned and jokes told will have you smiling, nodding, rolling your eyes, shaking your head and groaning at the same time. The final chapter, *Short Shorts* and *Strange Things* (and terrible jokes) is worth the price of the book in itself!"

—**Jane Jackson**, author, ***Navigating Career Crossroads***

Never Do Anything Just Right

A Mile Down the Road and a Half

Rod Jahner

Never Do Anything Just Right

> → A Mile Down the Road and a Half

Copyright © 2022 by Rod Jahner

All rights reserved. Except as permitted under the U.S. Copyright Act of 1976, no part of this publication may be reproduced, distributed, or transmitted in any form by any means, or stored in a database or retrieval system, without the prior written permission of the publisher.

No money or other payment has been received from any person, company, or other entity in exchange for any mention or lack thereof in this book.

Except where noted, names have not been changed to protect the supposedly innocent.

Or the more honest, either.

Cover and back cover photos by Rod Jahner.

Cover design by Marc de Celle

Author photo on last page by Cindy Jahner

Just Rod Books

First Edition, Second Printing, October 2022

ISBN 979-8-218-06287-3

For Dad,
whose love of life, work ethic,
wanderlust (largely unrealized)
and natural gift with kids inspires
me to this day, more than half a
century after his passing.

For Mom,
the quintessential supermom
before the term was conceived, who
regretted not keeping a paper she wrote in
high school chronicling the story of her family's
fascinating life through the eyes of her father.
She inspired me to write my own, in the hope
that those who follow might find a bit
of insight, and a laugh or two.

→ Table of Contents

	Introduction	1
Chapter One	Early Life in Linton	5
Chapter Two	Life in Bismarck	21
Chapter Three	Single Life in Denver	53
Chapter Four	Family Life in St. Louis	75
Chapter Five	Life at the Beach	91
Chapter Six	Life Adventures in Singapore	99
Chapter Seven	A Good Life in North Carolina	135
Chapter Eight	Gone to a Better Life	153
Chapter Nine	Life Lessons 101A: Airlines and Stupidity	169
Chapter Ten	Life Lessons 101B: Don't Do That	175
Chapter Eleven	Life Lessons 101C: Short Shorts & Strange Things	181
	Bookend	191
	Epilogue of Gratitude	193

Introduction

→ For Family. But you can join in.

After a lifetime re-telling some of the cocktail party classics, gathering new material, traveling more than a trivial amount, and wanting to fill a bucket list desire to have my name on a book, here goes.

This is for family. I would give pretty much anything to have recollections in the words of my parents, who emerged from the Greatest Generation with a humility and work ethic that belied their power of endurance through difficult, simple, and still amazing formative years.

As for this book, it will sell at least two copies, maybe three if someone other than me actually feels an urge to buy one. (If you're not family but you buy a copy, consider yourself an adjunct member.) The two copies in my possession are for sons Kyle and Corey, tales of whom, amongst a lot of other dribble, are sprinkled throughout these pages. My guess is that they won't really appreciate the effort until after I'm gone and they have gained the sentimentality that comes from a life that is more behind than in front of them. Much like I feel at the moment.

Some time ago I was advised to write this, by a sage of a friend who surmised, "It's already written." I reflected on those words not long after being gifted with four spanking-new stents, thanks to the modern medicine that could have lengthened my dad's life considerably, if only the advances had come decades sooner. He passed at 63 years of age, and I've already outlived him by a number of years. Mom almost made 97. Guess which genes I'm hoping for? Well, somewhere in between, anyway. The time bad habits take away (don't you know drinking will take 1.35 years off of your life?) comes at the end, and those years stink anyway.

Another source of inspiration is my ever-creative daughter-in-law Leigh, who asked my wife Cindy and I to each write an annual letter to our grandkids on their birthdays, all of which will be sealed and opened at an age of appreciation. Genius. After writing the first ones, I so look forward to the rest. Again, if only I had such a gift from my grandparents.

So where to begin? For some time now I've been creating lists. The best of those cocktail stories. Favorite jokes. Writings by Son 1, Kyle the journalist, who has a gift for dissecting complex problems and creating reasonable arguments for a solution. Tales of Son 2, Corey, now an attorney and a redefinition of raising *The Strong-Willed Child* (Cindy bought that book when he was six months old). A speech here and there. Collections of short stories recalling favorite memories of friends who left this Earth far too soon, intended to provide a laugh or a bit of comfort to loved ones left behind, but turning out to be more therapeutic for me. A wide range of memories, from growing up in North Dakota to living abroad for the ten-year adventure of our lives. Fun times with my only sibling, Al, six years older than me, who put up with and tortured me in our early days, and then became such a close friend as we grew into adulthood. A wonderful extended family. A small-world story (actually two) that I challenge anyone to top. Loads of interesting friends who actually put up with a sense of humor that is, at the least, caustic, and at times, just plain demented. And other stuff sprinkled in for good measure as it comes to mind.

Brother Al accused me of writing a book so I could have gifts for the family which I don't have to pay for. That is categorically false. Although he did just talk himself into his next present.

Cindy has the same cutting sense of humor I possess. Quick on the trigger, you always know where you stand, a quality that magnificently compliments my all-too-often methodical decision-making. Together we have ruined our two sons. They had no chance. Examples are strewn throughout these pages, and are contributing factors to the title of the book—but more on that later. As for "A Mile Down the Road and a Half", it's a colloquialism from North Dakota that has stuck with me. I remember it being said in a heavy German brogue when referencing distance. "Yah, that's about a mile down the road and a half." But don't over-elongate the 'Yah' like the Coen brothers did in the movie Fargo. That was just wrong. You've had your first German brogue lesson. You're welcome.

This is for the boys to hold on to for their kids. I'll give the third copy to Cindy. Al's present is now secure. For reasons I don't understand, my hairdresser wants a copy.

Do I hear six?

Chapter One

→ Early Life in Linton

Where?

I was born in Linton, North Dakota on August 6, 1953. A booming metropolis of around 2,000 residents supporting the local farming community, today reduced to scarcely half that population. The raised eyebrows continue to appear whenever I announce my North Dakota roots. "I've never met anyone from North Dakota." "You're the first." "I've never been there." "It's really cold there isn't it?" Big surprise, no surprise, really no surprise and, yes, respectively. Although the saying that we have nine months of winter and three months of bad sledding is just a bit of an exaggeration. (I may live in North Carolina—not Dakota—now, but I reserve the right to use the inclusive *we* when it comes to my home state.)

In the state's centennial year (1989), a legislative committee actually voted in favor of dropping "North" from the name of the state, as Dakota would not sound so cold. The governor of South Dakota at the time suggested that if they wanted to make it sound warmer, "they ought to call it Tallahassee."

My parents both grew up on farms. Large families with eight siblings on Mom's side and thirteen on Dad's, which would eventually generate around a hundred first cousins alone. Needed to make those farm hands. And be good Catholics (Pope says you've got to do it). The growth of the state can be largely attributed to the Homestead Act of 1862 under President Lincoln, which allowed "the head of a household (a man or woman) over the age of 21 to claim 160 acres of land and receive title to the land after living on the land for five years and improving the land by cultivating it and building a home." This swelled the state's population to around 680,000 by 1930, which remained the state's high point for the next eighty years, after an exodus during the Dust Bowl of the '30s. Only in the last twenty years, thanks mostly to the oil boom in the Bakken Shale, has the state's population grown to a level representing more than ten people per square mile. Thanks to oil discovery and fracking technology, North Dakota now pumps more of the black stuff out of the ground than any other state except Texas, having recently passed Alaska, Oklahoma and California. Most are surprised at that little revelation. All of that said, I'm not sure if there will ever be a million people up there. Still a couple hundred thousand away from that milestone. At this point I'm sure you have a burning desire to immediately divert to Wikipedia for more fun facts on North Dakota. (I'll wait.)

That didn't take long. Life in Linton was as simple as you might expect. Both parents worked, lots of family in the area, independence at a young age playing in the neighborhood with friends, just making up stuff to do. Very safe environment. Today when I drive by the house in which I started this life, it looks so small—but didn't seem to be at the time. When I was seven and eight years old, I spent a couple of weeks each summer on Uncle Ed and

Aunt Carol's farm, 'helping' them. I took particular delight seated between Uncle Ed's legs on the little Massey Ferguson tractor used as the runabout for small jobs. A quarter of a century later we would visit that same farm with our boys when they were two and four. They each rode with Uncle Ed on that same tractor.

With a few friends, I went to my first horror movie when I was in second grade. No idea the title, but I vividly remember the canopy on the four-poster bed slowly lowering as it devoured the occupant who could have—let me think—rolled out of bed. We walked the six blocks home in the middle of the street (it was now dark) to avoid any danger that lurked. A brave lot we were.

Dad

Dad was born in this country on a farm near one of many small farm towns, this one called Strasburg. Strasburg is a hop, skip and a jump away from Linton. On another farm in the area was one Lawrence Welk who would go on to fame for his musical variety show, retaining forever his German brogue. Dad told us of going to barn dances when Welk was starting out. Welk's own family would tell him "go back to the farm, Larry, you can't make any money playing music." Lawrence Welk's 'champagne music' show would be televised for over 30 years and syndication reruns have never stopped. He traded the farm for a golf membership in Palm Springs.

As Dad grew up, he would attend barber school and move off the farm. By WWII he was in his mid-30s (born 1906) so his military service would be stateside assisting wounded warriors on their return from battle. A couple of years ago I purchased bricks for him and my brother Al, a Navy vet, commemorating their service at the new military monument at Sunset Beach, North Carolina. He would never have seen that coming; I hope he likes it near the intercoastal waterway. Dad had a bit of wanderlust that I would embrace in my 30s—more on that later. Suffice to say he wanted out of Linton, and set his sights on the big city, Bismarck (around 20,000 residents back in the day), where better educational opportunities awaited his boys. He married Mom in 1942, barbered in Linton, then ran the local hardware store before his return to barbering. I remember his hands were always impeccably manicured (by himself) and he always kept peppermint chews by the bagful near his barber chair, both habits designed to ensure his customers were never offended by his appearance nor bad breath. By the way, he had a good Catholic name: Pius. There were lots of them in the Dakotas in those days, not so much today. The four-chair barbershop Dad worked in was owned by another Pius. My guess is you've never met a Pius. I knew or was related to about six of them.

My dad was not a large man by any means. Stood all of 5'6", but always seemed much taller by the way he carried himself. Worked hard all his life, and helped others at every turn. When he wasn't on his feet all day cutting hair at the barbershop (I sported a flat-top held in place by Butch Wax; you could land small aircraft on it), he was at the hospital cutting hair as needed for free. He was a joiner and participant, holding memberships in multiple fraternal organizations including the Knights of Columbus, Veterans of Foreign Wars (VFW), American Legion, and Lions. I still have the pins from all of them. He was a snappy dresser within the budget allowed, and for some time I have worn many of his cufflinks, now in excess of 70 years old. Later in life Mom would make Christmas stockings from scraps of material, some of which include pieces removed from his old neckties. We hang those stockings every year to this day.

He could whistle, without any assistance from placing fingers in the mouth, and be heard for blocks. All Dad had to do was put his head out of the door and whistle, at which time his boys had better drop whatever they were doing or playing with, and come home for supper. On the run. After yelling "Coming!"

He was also a visionary. When helping set up fireworks displays, for instance, he would admonish organizers to fire off the individual cannisters in much more rapid succession than was ever done at the time. Today all displays do so. When the Bismarck Civic Center was first built in 1969, holding far more people for events than anything around at the time (over 5,000 seats, which I installed quite a few of as a laborer), he immediately said it was too small. Today the capacity of the renamed Bismarck Event Center is 10,100, having been expanded long ago.

Finally, Dad was a kid magnet. He was like a pied piper when little ones were around; they loved him and laughed from their ankles at his antics. Thankfully I acquired a small part of that, along with many other nuances that comfortably stay with me.

He left this world far too early in 1969, a few weeks before what would have been his 63rd birthday and having been married to Mom for 27 years. With the significant generation gap, I was 16 and a junior in high school. Too young to appreciate him as I should have; but I have done so since.

Today I carry his rosary every day and pray it more religiously than I have in prior years. I have a ring he wore that matches a pair of his old cufflinks, a nice combination for special occasions, like my boys' weddings. A small diamond and the gold from another ring found their way to a re-do of my wife's wedding ring. A bit of him stays with me all the time, perhaps with a bit more nostalgia than ever. The mementos will be passed on to my boys, who I hope someday appreciate them a fraction as much as I do today.

Mom

Mom was born in Russia in 1912 (Celestine but always Sally to, let me see, everyone), the first of the many in the Julius and Elizabeth Deis family. In 1913, just after her first birthday, the three of them immigrated to the U.S., like so many Germans from Russia, who would populate what became known as "The Sauerkraut Triangle"—a vast farming area surrounding Bismarck, stretching approximately between Dickinson and Rugby, North Dakota, and Aberdeen, South Dakota, comprising nearly 20,000 square miles. This was Homestead Act land, on a similar latitude to the Russian land Germans had peacefully farmed for over a hundred years thanks to relaxed rules of the eighteenth-century Czars. Immigrants knew the crops that thrived in the similar climate.

We have the ship's manifest (the Bremen) from Ellis Island archives, along with a picture and some added knowledge from our visit there. On one of the pages of the handwritten manifest are their three names, along with a variety of other information. Grandpa had $500 in his pocket, a considerable sum for the time. Authorities wanted immigrants to have at least $50 so they could subsist for six months. As the story goes, they left considerable wealth behind, unable to take anything out of the country other than some cash and clothing. Grandma smuggled her favorite candy dish in a suitcase. My brother has it to this day, with its beautiful blue color and tiger embossed on the bottom. My keepsake is the family passport, issued to the three of them in Russian, along with the cloth folio which contained the valuable document. The folio has a picture of the Bremen on the front.

The three of them joined others from the family already in North Dakota and began working the land. Built a sod home to start with. Used a cable spool for a dining room table. Grew crops that thrived in the familiar latitude. Mom would, later in life, talk about the paper she wrote in high school based on the considerable recollections and adventures of her dad, then immediately wish she had kept it. Another reason for this work.

One story that did endure was about Mom's Uncle Robert. One day at midnight he was 'volunteered' into the Red Army by the Bolsheviks, the majority faction founded by Vladimir Lenin and Alexander Bogdanov that split from the Menshevik faction of the Marxist Russian Social Democratic Labor Party, a revolutionary socialist political party formed in 1898. After forming their own party in 1912, the Bolsheviks took power in Russia in November 1917, overthrowing the liberal Provisional Government of Alexander Kerensky, and became the only ruling party in the subsequent Soviet Russia and its successor regime, the Soviet Union. This was not exactly the career path Uncle Robert foresaw. Years after he disappeared into the army, and after the family had emigrated, Robert would go AWOL, escape across country and over barbed wire fences, find his way to England, then to the U.S., and finally to North Dakota. The long-awaited and tearful reunion began when Mom was playing with a cousin on the farm and they saw him walking up the road.

The greatest escape of my life involved a scarf, an inebriated patron of a local bar and an assist from a very large friend. The full story is no comparison to my Great Uncle Robert, so I'll just stop.

Another of the stories Cindy and I resurrected with a trip to Ellis Island was on the Bremen's ship manifest. I have a copy which lists the particulars of Mom and the two grandparents. The curator who worked with us at Ellis pointed out the date 6-21-41 handwritten in the nationality column of my grandfather's line item, above the original entry 'Russian.' She advised us that this date documented my grandfather's naturalization as a U.S. citizen, and it would have been entered via notification of the event from the county courthouse in North Dakota.

The hard copy of the ship's 1903 manifest had not only endured at Ellis, but information from county records in North Dakota had found its way back to update the manifest more than 27 years after Mom and her parents arrived in America.

Another 70 years after that, I still can't go to a new doctor's office without replaying every detail of medical history and prescriptions for the umpteenth time. Seems to me that in our electronic age we should be just a touch better at recordkeeping.

Mom would be the first in the family to go to college. Like all of her siblings, male or female, she worked on the farm. Not wanting to be an obvious farmer to her classmates (the dead giveaway being a good tan) she would wear long sleeves, a big hat, gloves and Ponds Cold Cream on her face held in place with flour to keep her skin light in color. This would prove to be a reasonably good idea later in life, as her skin always belied her age. College brought a teaching degree, whereupon Mom returned to live at home and teach all eight grades in a one-room schoolhouse. Everyone has heard the joke about how their parents walked two miles, through the snow, uphill (both directions) to get to work. Wasn't a joke with Mom; she did that, minus the uphill both directions part. Grandpa would give her a ride if it was really cold. (I never knew the temperature threshold for a ride, but it must have been similar to the one set for me in grade school: If well below zero, I'd get a ride instead of taking the nine-block walk.) Mom would be sure to arrive at the schoolhouse before the kids to fire up the stove, warm the place up, and, I'm not making this up, thaw out the ink bottles. One day she left the inks on top of the stove for too long whereupon they exploded, creating quite a mess on the walls. She and Grandpa would go back that weekend and repaint. Just another day in the country for these tough people.

Mom would go on to a professional career at JC Penney, as credit manager for their Bismarck store. She was the original super-mom, like all of our moms at the time. Worked full time, cooked, cleaned, just went on and on without complaint. She would live to be almost 97, kicking cancer to the curb at 89 with geriatric chemo (well, one dose, anyway—all of her hair came out and it almost killed her, so that was the end of that), then radiation for six weeks. Cancer, gone. Four years later she had a small stroke and heart attack, and after a pacemaker was installed would be back in her assisted living room doing crafts by the end of the week. Son Kyle would observe, "Dad, that's the big three: cancer, stroke and heart attack. Even God can't take Grandma."

Mom and Dad met in Linton and eventually married in 1942, but Mom did not want children until after the war. Didn't want to be a widow with a family to raise on her own. Really Mom? Dad was 36 years old, well beyond age of deployment to the trenches, and working in a hospital in Alabama. What were the odds of you losing him to WWII?

Mom's craft work was a part of her for as long as I can remember, and continued until she began losing her eyesight well into her nineties. She was very talented, donated thousands of items to the church for sales while selling others herself. From blankets to crochet work, designer eggs to bookmarks, she was creative and prolific. I once asked her for party favors of crocheted bookmarks in a flamingo theme, sent her the pictures and she turned around 50 of them inside of a couple weeks. Her NOEL sign hangs in our home every Christmas, the product of hand sewing hundreds of tiny sequins into the phrase. And we cherish the hand-sewn Christmas stockings. In times of stress the simple lighting of her candle brings solace. Doesn't get much better.

Big Brother Al

Allen James Jahner was born in 1946 (Mom and Dad waited until 1953 for me). He would tell you that they had created perfection so there was no incentive to have another for quite some time, if ever. (I have an entirely different opinion.) Early years growing up was a bit more like being two only-kids than close siblings, given the six plus years of separation. He was the big brother I idolized, a natural athlete at just about anything he tried. I loved sports, tried everything and was always far more competitive than talented. Very frustrating way to live.

Al was my protector when he wasn't finding a way to torment me. When I was six, he was two blocks from home when he heard my screams; I had been stung just below the eye by a bumblebee. He came running and found me crying in the driveway, with the bee dead at my feet. My eye swelled up like a tick at a blood bank, and I was allowed the rare treat of staying inside to watch cartoons with the good eye while healing. Outside was where kids belonged, and where every possible moment was spent, largely unsupervised, just playing every game we could think of with friends. Until Dad whistled us home.

Expectations needed to be reset on rare occasions. In a lasting fashion. The only time I remember this happening, I was around seven years old, so Al would have been in his teens—when he received a few strokes from the razor strap, a tool of Dad's barber trade. This was a three-foot-long, four-inch-wide and around one-quarter-inch-thick piece of solid leather, with an equal-sized piece of woven burlap attached at the top, used to sharpen and hone straight-edge razors. Said another way, one solid hunk of 'Oh My Dear God in Heaven' for any clear-thinking adolescent, with a strap of burlap right behind it. On this occasion it was used to administer a bit of discipline. I can still hear the slap-slap of the leather followed by the burlap connecting with big brother's posterior. After just hearing the sound, for the next two years I was **good**. Much later in life I would find that old razor strap, have it shadow-box framed and give it to Al for one of his birthdays. He wasn't as thrilled at receiving as I was at the act of giving.

Al shared his love of sports with me, and was my first coach. In baseball, though I am right-handed with everything, he had me bat left-handed. His reasoning was that most pitchers are right-handed, and their curve balls would break into you, as opposed to away, an advantage for the batter. Another advantage is being a step or two closer to first base. Which he would later let me know would be necessary given my less than blinding speed. Thanks a bunch.

He taught me the value of practice. When he introduced me to golf, he showed me his practice routine at a deserted green in the middle of nowhere in Bismarck, ND. Most of the time he had the area to himself, would take 50-60 balls, hit from various distances and before retrieving them, practice chipping from where the errant shots landed. Once all balls were on the green, they were scooped up and taken back to a different approach distance. He always had a natural golf swing.

Al served in the Navy during the Vietnam years, having failed to cram a four-year college degree into, let me see, four years. It was the draft or join and he joined. He was in pretty good company in that regard. His tour would include one obligatory six-month assignment to the Far East; the rest of the time was spent in Southern California.

Once back in California, he honed that already natural golf swing with every opportunity. Disgustingly smooth with a golf club and I not so secretly hated him with every fiber of my being for it. I play with him once a year or so to remind myself why I don't do it more often. The real reason is geography. Unfortunately, Sunset Beach, NC is not exactly handy to Santa Fe, NM.

Tacos and the Big City

When I was in second grade, Mom and Dad were looking to move from Linton to Bismarck, which was at the time, in 1960, more than ten times the size of Linton. Okay, population 25,000, but really big to us. Would it help to relay that today the city has 80,000 inhabitants? Probably not.

One of my best friends at the time, and still a close friend to this day, was Randy, whose dad, Pete, owned a furniture and carpeting business. Pete also wanted to move to a larger market. I would find out much later in life (blissfully unaware as a child I suppose) that Pius and Pete had commuted together for almost two years. For 63 miles each way, 126 miles round-trip, between Linton and Bismarck, each day. Dad had found a job barbering and Pete was working on setting up his Magi-Touch home store, today in its third generation as a family-run business. And both looking for housing that would fit their family's needs. One day on the way back to Linton, Dad would announce to Pete, "I bought a house today." And so, it was time to move. I was between second and third grade.

The house was, in a word, modest. The critical elements of location and affordability for which Dad had been searching for months, finally found. Two bedrooms, one bath, living room, kitchen large enough for the only dining table, utility room for the washer/dryer and storage, and a one-car detached garage. With an apartment in the basement that was nearly the same size, rented out to help pay the mortgage. There was a small cellar downstairs for Mom's canned jams, vegetables and of course, homemade pickles. Everything was homemade. Go out to eat? Why? To this day Al and I are still trying to duplicate some of those recipes, which for the most part weren't written down; when asked how something was made, Mom would reply, "a little of this and a little of that." She was so good in the kitchen it was a miracle we could fit through the door. But Al and I were blessed with fast metabolisms and ate anything and everything without gaining weight. In high school I set the A&B Pizza record for most tacos in a sitting. Fifteen. I weighed in at around a buck and a quarter at the time. Didn't stay that way in later life.

Some of the favorites at the dinner table? Friday was fried dumpling night. Fresh sausage from Uncle Ed's farm on Sunday mornings. Blueberry muffins. Pancakes that were twice the thickness of any you ever saw. Liver and onions. (Yes, I just said that. Cut thin, fried and smothered with sautéed onions.) The first TV dinners I ever liked: Throughout the year, Mom would save the aluminum containers from TV dinners we had purchased and consumed; then, the day after Thanksgiving, out they would come: mashed potatoes and gravy in one small compartment, veggies in the other, and a boatload of turkey, dressing and gravy in the large compartment. Then stacked nicely in the always full, chest-deep freezer, which always had enough food to get us through a winter or four. Baked goods galore. Good old German kuchen. And the topper of all, her homemade caramel rolls. Warm with butter melted on them, my God in heaven they were epic. Her Grandson Corey would later in life, after contracting diabetes, say that those rolls were worth risking his health.

Dad and I would always risk our health with an evening snack that consisted of fresh bread dipped in a half-and-half mix of homemade chokecherry jam and heavy farm cream. Life-changing. And you could hear the arteries slamming shut while eating.

I do not remember Mom ever sitting through a single one of her wonderful meals. She was constantly up and down, back and forth to the kitchen bringing piping hot seconds of everything, and encouraging thirds.

At the end of the day we didn't have much, didn't know we didn't have much, ate very, very well, learned a work ethic by example and assignment, and grew up in a small-town environment that was in retrospect pretty special. In grade school I was the classic nerd, always A's with the occasional B, math being my first love. After school there was playtime that canvassed the entire town, as long as you returned ON TIME. We were expected to be outside, summer and winter, and we happily complied. Oh, and there were regular chores as well. *Before* playtime.

Chapter Two

→ Life in Bismarck

Our modest home was in a handy location, imperative for a one car, two working parent family. One block to St. Mary's Central High School where Al was attending, nine blocks to Cathedral Grade School where I was in third grade, ten blocks from the barber shop for Dad and twelve to J.C. Penney for Mom. We all walked often, although given Mom's workload she was generally afforded a ride to work.

Solid friendships developed early, with my old friend Randy from Linton moving to Bismarck soon after we did, and new friends Mike, Glen, Bill and Denny all within a few blocks of our new house.

Randy's family would stay very close to the Jahners through the years. He would eventually take over the family business, the Magi-Touch home store, grow it substantially and bring in his twin boys as the third generation of hard-working success.

My new friend Mike was in the middle of a family of 13 kids. Going to his house was a marvel of movement, with his mom in a perpetual state of cooking, cleaning and laundry. His father Earl was a lifelong bricklayer, who upon retirement sat in his easy chair and didn't move enough to keep a self-winding watch running. (This was a proven fact through testing: The watch ran perfectly for two different sons whenever they wore it. Earl could then make it stop.)

Glen's dad, Alex, was one of the funniest men I'd ever met, and later in my life would be the tipping point that landed me a job at Job Service of North Dakota, launching a series of fascinating career moves. Glen would turn out to be the athlete among us, an excellent linebacker on the gridiron and catcher on the baseball field. Glen and I have stayed close enough to call each other on our birthdays to this day.

Bill's dad owned a local supermarket and they lived in a brick house, so they must have been rich.

Denny would go on to be a prison warden and, interestingly enough, would at one point have a former classmate as one of his guests.

At the end of the day we had a simple, mostly untethered life. School was the priority, of course. Leisure time was spent at the local pool in the summer or on a sled in the winter. Lots of bike riding all over the city and to recreation on the Missouri River, which bordered the west side of town. We spent the majority of our time with kids from our Catholic school, and later would develop relationships with some from the cross-town rival public school, or even kids from the sister city of Mandan, across the river.

Pat was another friendship which would endure. I first met him in grade school, where his dad Dave was teaching and starting a wrestling team. His was a family of wrestlers. It just so happened that Pat and I were the same weight class, so we worked out together. No wrestling tights in those days, so we wore long john underwear under a pair of gym shorts. It was in this ensemble that Pat would give me multiple views of the ceiling in the Cathedral Grade School gymnasium. It got to the point that I knew the number of ceiling tiles in that place. Pat would go on to be a state wrestling champion in high school. Later in life I would remind him that I was his competitive launching pad. An idea that never quite took hold.

We decided to try football, where creative drills involved lining us up with partners 50 yards apart, one the 'runner' and the other the 'tackler'. The jobs of both were to run directly at the other at full speed, not veering. The full speed direct contact created a nice violent collision that would never be replicated in any game. Then do it again. And again. That same coaching genius would try me out at fullback after I ran for a touchdown in practice. A few plays later, after missing a block, I suddenly found myself dangling in midair, as he grabbed me by the butt and neck, lifted me and shook me up and down while yelling at me for my mistake. No instruction followed, but I was mercifully moved to the bench—where I would stay. Much later in life I would commission the Singapore American Football League, where we had a better balance of instruction, design of drills and a far smaller dose of ridicule from our coaches. Funny how some things come full circle.

Basketball started in grade school as well. Our first coaches would have such useful drills as lining us all up against a wall and throwing balls at us, at random, overhand pretty much as hard as they could. Supposed to teach us reflexes. It taught me sprained fingers and, let me think, *fear*. The next coach had us jump rope before practice, starting at a few hundred reps and by the end of the season, 2,000 per day. Glen and I were roping partners and were pretty good at it. Great conditioning, gave us some "hops" for rebounding on the court, but did nothing for a decided lack of height and natural basketball talent.

In the summer the pool was our haven, and with a Dairy Queen next door, not much was wrong in the world. Denny's family would later take me along for the short drive from Bismarck to Miami, Florida where his dad had a convention. At the hotel pool the challenge was to learn each other's signature dives. I could complete a 1½ front flip but could not do a back flip. Denny the opposite. After about a half hour of him completing 1¼'s and me perfecting the ¾ back flip we finally got it right. Much to the relief of our reddened beat up stomachs, thanks to the flops.

That talent thing (or lack thereof) mentioned earlier suited my early sports prowess to a tee. But never did I lose my enthusiasm for playing something with a ball, sliding down a hill, skating, biking, whatever. I like to think that I passed this love on to my boys, both of whom had more athletic success than their father (the talent thing apparently skips a generation) and who, much to their mother's chagrin, are still playing rugby in their 30's. Between the three of us we've had multiple knee surgeries (dad), a broken jaw (Corey, rugby, "it was just a freak accident, Mom"), dislocated collar bone (Kyle, rugby, I didn't know you could even do that, and he hates this line but he will never be able to wear a strapless gown), a pinky fingerprint that popped off from a pitched baseball smashing his little finger against a bat, a big toe bone split the *long* way catching (Kyle, baseball, also didn't know you could do either of those), two broken collar bones (Corey thanks to Dad and Corey again, football), and who knows how many cuts glued shut and/or compression bandaged (both boys - after all, the rugby game must go on). Just to name a few.

I have one friend who asked "Could you guys just list the stuff you have NOT had?"

But I digress. Back in Bismarck we worked hard, played hard and developed enduring friendships. Doesn't get much better than that.

The Eaves and other Chores

As I grew old enough, the lawn mowing, leaf raking, hedge trimming and shoveling became my expectation. By now Al was off to college and I was nearing the end of grade school. The shoveling was mind-numbing and, most of the time, hands-and feet-numbing. And glasses constantly fogging. The sidewalks on this small house were, in a word, ridiculous. Pull shovel from garage, clear the walk to the house, up and down a double staircase at the back door, shovel the landing, then around the house in front of the basement apartment and on to the front steps, thirteen of them, then out to the front walkway and finally clear the walkway across the front. Done yet? Not so fast. Now back to the garage, shovel around it and then push all the snow across the double driveway and throw it over a four-foot fence into our backyard. Now you're done. An inch or two was a chore. More was a couple of hours. Throw in a blizzard and you have your day's entertainment. I used a metal push shovel for most of the work, about two feet wide. Over the years I wore about eight inches of metal off of that shovel. Much later in life, when Al and I were clearing out the parent's home, he would grant me the joy of throwing that damn shovel off the back of the pickup at the junkyard. Happiest day of my life to that point was watching it glisten in the sun as it flipped end over end into the trash heap.

While we're on the subject of chores, if you would like to see my sons' eyes roll, just mention the word "eaves." When I was still in grade school, I spent the better part of six weeks one fine summer on a ladder, scraping and painting the eaves on our house. Dad gave me twenty bucks and I thought I was as rich as I ever would be. Believe I've told that story one (hundred or so) times too many to the boys. "Did I ever tell you the story about the eaves?"

Eyes and Teeth—Sorry I'm Not Sorry

My eyes were myopic beyond myopic. Each year brought a new pair of glasses, stronger than the last. When riding my bike home with newfound vision, the feeling was that I was ten feet off of the ground while getting used to the drastic change in prescription. Over time, without correction, these eyes were bringing me closer to legal blindness. Actually, if you go by the World Health Organization definitions, I bypassed legally blind and moved onto 'profound visual impairment' and eventually 'near total blindness.' I would go on to hold the record for visual *dis*acuity at my ophthalmologist's office in St. Louis for a number of years. Another vision professional would grade my vision without correction at "20/Forget It." At one point, after a few too many adult beverages the night before, I would ask, and by ask I mean beg my roommate not to leave the apartment until we, and by we I meant he, could find my glasses. Peaked at 13 diopters for those of you who are eye geeks. For those who are not familiar with the measurement, I could read the 'E' on top of the chart because I knew it was the first letter they were going to point to. When we moved to Asia, I removed my contacts at my first eye exam, they put up the chart and I said my usual "E." The doctor said "No, it's a 5." To which I would reply, "What do you mean it's a 5? It's been an E for 40 years. That's not fair."

Enough of the eyes. Let's talk teeth. Another reason my parents never had money. When my baby teeth were being replaced by the permanent variety, my right upper central incisor (your front tooth for those of you who don't want to Google for that little tidbit like I did) came in deformed, in a shape that can only be described as a bowling pin. Not the look my parents were hoping for. So it was pulled and believe it or not, saved by Mom. I still have the little relic to this day. Just a bit creepy according to my wife. The prospect was then to wait for all the teeth to mature and insert a bridge and artificial tooth so I could effectively eat apples without cutting them up and, this is important, not leave behind a row of corn on the cob for the rest of my life. Oh, and take a decent picture. Then an odd thing happened, at least according to the dental knowledge of the day. A third tooth appeared in the same spot, the actual permanent tooth, shaped properly. That's the good news. The bad news was that it arrived at a perfect 90 degree angle. Hello braces. Three different times. The first set straightened the tooth over about a year. Then a retainer that had no chance. Tooth returns to its crooked state, braces again, And the process repeated itself a final time. I would learn early on much about my threshold of pain, which the sadist that we called a dentist would seek and find with every adjustment. Tighten those babies with a pliers until I couldn't take it. Then send me home to wait for the next opportunity a few weeks down the line.

Wonderful. The all-metal technology was a magnet for everything. Starting with food and proceeding to my personal favorite, any errant ball from any game of any kind within a three-block radius, square in the mouth. The inside of that mouth was hamburger for years.

Fast forward to Son 2, Corey, at a similar age. When his first dental x-rays were taken the dentist expressed surprise to Cindy that he had an extra tooth, looking much like a bowling pin, coming in through the roof of his mouth, behind the incisors. Cindy's response, "Yeah, we've done that." He would also go on to have braces twice (much better technology, chose his colors each adjustment, piece of cake compared to the old man so quit complaining son). Then his eyes started going as well, but a visionary ophthalmologist (the same one with whom I held the office *dis*acuity record) would put him in hard contact lenses very early on, with the theory that the myopia could be at least partially arrested. Which it was, and his sight never would deteriorate like his dad's.

Later in life, Corey would express his gratitude for the gifts that I, through heredity, would bestow upon the lucky lad. Bowling pin tooth, myopia, receding hair line to name the big three. Does he give me any credit whatsoever for his athleticism? Or that snappy sense of humor? No.

Gopher Firing Squad

My dad taught me to shoot a rifle when I was around eight years old. From the open window of a car. I am not making this up. Actually, it was very safe. Uncle Matt had a farm we visited fairly regularly. Insert oddity here: Uncle Matt was my father's brother and married to one of Mom's sisters. So their kids were as first as cousins get. Back to the safety thing, which I'm sure you are doubting.

Uncle Matt had a problem with gophers on one particular part of the farm. Hundreds of them in a colony of diggers and, as it turns out, not-too-bright congregators. They stood on a hillside in groups of two or three outside of their holes. Dad pulled the car right up to the hill, about ten feet away from the congregation. Not a gopher moved.

I was in the passenger seat. Dad calmly put me through the paces, teaching me how to shoot.

Window down (good plan), with the single shot 22 caliber rifle balanced on the sill. Insert one bullet at a time, move it into the chamber with the bolt action, then pull back the manual firing pin, release the safety, aim and fire. And miss. And miss. And miss again. And finally hit one. Here's where the not-too-bright part comes in. If you shoot a gopher in a tight grouping, you would expect his little buddies to head for cover. Not so with these guys. The others simply continued their conversation, waiting for their own fate. Personally I think they were suicidal. Might as well have put a blindfold on each of them and handed out little cigarettes. There really isn't much use for gophers in the ecosystem of a farm, and a 22 gives a more painless way out than any gopher ever gets at the hand of nature.

Later in life I, like many of my friends, would graduate to other forms of hunting. I was mainly an upland game (grouse, partridge, etc.) and duck hunter. There are a few stories that deserve their own section later. We always stayed within established limits, happily paid whatever fees necessary for the privilege to participate, and never, ever wasted what we harvested. With the possible exception of those gophers. They didn't look too appetizing.

On a business trip one day in New York (I lived in Denver at the time), a dyed-in-the-wool native asked me where I grew up. When I replied North Dakota, she looked down her nose at me and this exchange followed:

Her: "What do you do for fun in a place like that?"

Me: "I play golf and fish, and in the fall we go duck hunting."

Her: "You mean you *actually shoot* them? Why would you do that?"

Me: "So that we can *actually eat* them."

My Last Toboggan Ride. Ever.

Here's a stunner: For fun in the North Dakota winter, we went sledding. Lots of rolling hills, alleys with a slope behind houses—anything that let gravity do its thing. One fine winter's day, my parents took friend Glen and me to the local golf course. (Like I said, anything un-flat enough for gravity to work.) There was a particular snow-covered hole on the course, an all-uphill par four, with about a 30% incline for a good 200 yards. So some considerable speed was possible, going green to tee—the wrong way, but there weren't any golfers around to complain or get in the way. We had a six foot toboggan that day and had made a couple of great runs.

On what would be the final run of the day, Glen fell off about halfway down the hill. Yours truly is left at the helm of this long plank of 'there is no way on God's green Earth that a single person of any strength can steer'. Might as well have been on railroad tracks. Oh, and there were trees around the bottom of the hill. Did I mention the speed thing?

Dad was at the top of the hill and Mom in the comfort of a warm car. I was careening directly toward a meeting with what would become my least favorite tree in the world. Unable to steer the planks of death, I bailed out just before the impending head-on collision. Physics lesson here: In the act of pushing away from the toboggan, it veered to safety. Momentum lesson next: My body continued on the same path, hitting the tree flush across my thighs at something just under light speed. Pain lesson now: For reasons that escaped us all, I did not break either leg, but this was not known at the time. Sure felt like it. Back on the hill my friend Glen, halfway down the hill when he ejected, started running toward me at full speed. He would later describe how he was moving fast and my 55-year-old, 5'6" father, who started at the top of the hill some 75 yards behind, went past him like he was standing still. The toboggan made a handy stretcher with which to drag my sorry butt back to the car. They had me covered from head to toe and as we approached, for a brief moment Mom thought I was dead. At the hospital it was determined that the leg bones were intact, but the thigh bruises were so deep they required hospitalization and therapy for four days.

Never rode a toboggan again.

Popularity Contest

I was a junior in high school when brother Al joined the Navy, avoiding the annoying jungles of Vietnam. Just before his six-month tour of the Far East on the USS Horne, he wrote and asked me to send him two of the largest bottles of maraschino cherries I could find, slightly altered: Drain all the cherry juice, my orders read. Replace with Jim Beam. Two bottles of 'cherries' thus cleared inspection easily.

My mission successfully completed, I went rooting through Al's stuff. I found an old photo ID which, at that point in our lives, bore a reasonable resemblance to yours truly. Which gave it a purpose, a new *raison d'être*: I could now buy beer posing as a much older version of 'myself.' Talk about improving your popularity. Do you have any idea how many parties a guy with the ability to bring alcohol was invited to? Kind of like hanging a pork chop around a kid's neck to get the dog to play with him.

After a number of successful purchases, I wandered into a small liquor store in the south end of Bismarck. As I placed my case of beer on the counter, the attractive young lady working there asked for my ID, which I produced. She looked at it, then at me, and asked me to remove my sunglasses. This was the very short conversation that ensued:

Her: "This is your brother."
Me: "Why do you think that?"
Her: "Because I dated him."
Me: "You're not going to sell me the beer, are you?"
Her: "Ah, no."
What are the odds?

Only took me about 30 years before I fessed up and told Al what I'd been doing while he was sailing the Far East, and what had happened at that liquor store. He was a bit stunned, to say the least, but enough time had passed that he immediately appreciated the humor of my little predicament.

Duck Hunting: We Ate Everything. *Almost.*

In the fall, it was time to put away the golf clubs and go hunting. We were upland game (grouse and partridge, mostly) and duck hunters. Upland game for the first couple of weeks of the season as a warmup, then settling into duck season. We were on one of the major southern migration flyways for ducks and geese.

I preferred duck to goose hunting, where the limits were 1-2 birds per day per hunter. Duck limits were generally five, one of which could be a hen and the rest drakes, with a two bird 'bonus' if they were either Blue-winged or Green-winged Teals, but only one of which could be a Green-winged teal. I defy anyone to tell the difference between Green- and Blue-winged teals in flight. The wing markings are about a two inch square and they fly by at about 60 mph. It was luck of the draw.

We ate everything we harvested and paid strict attention to the rules. For years a rotating group of three of us hunted out of Fast Eddie's (I'll leave Ed's nickname to your own vivid imagination) banana yellow Chevy Luv pickup, with just enough space in the bed under the tarp for decoys, guns, waders, and the like. And not nearly enough room for the three of us across the bench seat at 4:30am, the necessary timing for legal shooting that began 30 minutes before sunrise at locations that were generally a 60-90 minute drive from town. In retrospect those were fun, a little insane, and fully-in-the-moment times. We loved them.

Every hunter has hundreds of stories. One of my favorites was the day, late in the season, where our favorite water locations were frozen over. So we drove toward larger and larger bodies of water, throwing rocks into each, looking for one where our rock didn't bounce. Finally struck liquid water at the Garrison Reservoir. There we set up, had a successful day and among others I brought down a merganser, a first for any of us. Huge duck. Roommate Pat would sometime later exclaim, "I've been hunting for 15 years and the first time I go out with these clowns we shoot a duck I'd never seen before. And Fast Eddie pulls out a book and has a name for the thing."

That day overlapped with the opening of deer season, apparent when a deer hunter was shooting at one that was swimming across the water less than 100 yards from our duck decoys. We changed from camo into orange hats, stood up out of our blinds and watched his futile efforts, his prey jumping out the other side and scampering away. The successful hunters would have their field-dressed prey tied out on top of their big SUVs for the drive home. We elected to be equally showy, centering our merganser on the tarp covering the full box of that tiny yellow pickup and tying its wings and feet to the four corners. When we pulled up beside one of those deer hunters back in town the look on his face was priceless. Oh, and that was the nastiest tasting thing I ever tried to eat. And I lived in Asia for ten years, land of some pretty interesting 'delicacies.' Turns out they are fish-eating ducks and their meat conveys their diet all too well.

There's one more duck-hunting story still to come, one of my favorites, in my tribute to Pat (rest his soul) in Chapter Eight. And if we ever meet for a beer, I'll tell you one of the best hunting dog jokes of all time.

Freshman Flushing (Wet Above the Ears)

Enter into St. Mary's Central High School in Bismarck, North Dakota, 1967, one green kid, excellent at classwork, with those very mediocre athletic skills and weighing in at just more than a pool cue. Enter also an opportunistic bully who always traveled with his posse. Not a good mix. He pretty much tormented me for the year, a push here, a pop there, with yours truly powerless to stop it. In retrospect I wish I had learned a bit of technique from someone, and executed just one punch to the nose. He was half again my size and would have wiped the floor with me, but at least there might have been a shred of dignity. Later in life when I had two boys of my own, the youngest Corey was similarly tormented at a much younger age, fourth grade if memory serves. His bully was similar size and I knew Corey was capable of taking care of himself. So I told him, "You may not start anything, but you have my permission to finish it. You might get in trouble at your (Catholic) school, but not at home." Sure enough a couple of weeks later I received the call from school. One punch and done. Problem never returned. Found myself envying him that. When I was satisfied with his action that day—after talking to and reminding him that the punishment for lying in our house was triple anything else—I sought out the school principal, an Irish Catholic nun. When I found her in the vestibule of the attached church, she matter-of-factly said "Well, we said we were going to let Corey take care of things and it looks like he did a pretty darn good job of it." I loved that woman.

Football. That'll toughen me up and garner respect. Two-a-day practices with full pads in 90+ degrees (yes it gets hot in North Dakota) were such a joy. In those days you were a wimp if you needed water. At the end of torture/practice we were each handed a pile of salt tablets to complete the dehydration process. About three weeks in I developed what later in life would be confirmed as ophthalmic migraines. My vision would have hazy lines of obstruction for a half hour or so, then disappear to be replaced by what only can be described as a saber sliding back and forth between the temples. One trip to the doctor and my football days were over. Which at the end of the day was a blessing in disguise, as I graduated high school at 5'11' and 135 lbs.; I would likely have been snapped like a twig at some point. My boys would enjoy considerably more success on the gridiron in their high school years, thanks to more natural ability and better coaching. To this day, they remember those men fondly who they will forever refer to as Coach. All of which pleased me greatly.

Basketball. Lots of trying and loving that game over the next three years. Rode a lot of pine (bench-sitting, for those not familiar). Began a career of playing defense against the starters every day as they worked on their plays. Defense I could play. Shooting the ball, bit more of a challenge. In spite of being a vertically-challenged forward with mediocre ball handling skills, I never lost the love of the game and played until near 30 years old. If I were to reincarnate, I'd add about a foot of height and a bit (ok a lot) more natural ability. I loved fighting for rebounds and driving the baseline. As it was, there was no demand whatsoever for a 5'11" power forward. Who knew?

Track & Field. Boring to some, but I always liked running. Wasn't strong enough for the field sports (discus, javelin, high jump, etc.) but made up for it by being slow on the track. I would settle into the half-mile (880 yards, akin to today's 800 meters) and run it in meets watching the winners from behind. Which reminds me of a story from an old friend about running the mile in a track meet. Four laps. When friends of his arrived late, showing up just at the end of the race, they found him running toe-to-toe with the leaders down the stretch and began to chant, "Go, go, go!" What they did not realize was that he was just completing his third lap as the leaders crossed the finish line. So, on he ran, one more lonely lap to go. I can relate.

Flushing. One fine tradition, a right-of-passage into high school, was having your head placed in a toilet bowl by a group of very respectable seniors, who then performed the flushing. If they didn't like you much, the bowl might not start out with clean water. In my case, my good friend Glen had an older brother, Greg, a senior who knew me well. He and a couple of accomplices approached me in the hall one day, and Greg observed rather matter-of-factly, "You know this has to happen. Don't fight it." I was compliant, relieved that I was his draw, and accompanied them willingly into the bathroom. They did a ceremonial at best, (perfectly clean) swirly, leaving only the top of my hair a bit wet. Piece of cake.

This memory would be revisited when Son 1, Kyle, came home from his freshman class when we lived in Singapore, calmly dropped his book bag and headed out. Turns out he was going to a boxing match with a senior named Calvin, across the street on top of a residential high rise. He lost. And gained a lot of respect. His mom thought he had a screw loose for not simply staying home. I got it. That experience would find its way into one of his writings on bullying in the school paper later. And be fondly remembered as a growth experience.

Funny how these things all come full circle.

The rest of the year is something of a blur. But then so is, at this point in my life, what I had for lunch yesterday.

Sophomore Javelin Dodging

Cross Country. We had a wonderful coach in cross country. Rather than train us on the terrain where events would take place, or anything like it for that matter, he would sit in a lawn chair in the shade and count laps as we ran around the block that housed the school and football/practice field. If you were of a personality type who found this level of involvement fulfilling, three words: Get. A. Life. Or three others: You chose unwisely. I dealt with the mind-numbing routine by memorizing geometry problems and solving them in my head as I droned on. Insert your own nerd joke here. Lost concentration one day and heard someone yelling at me, only to look up and see, about 15 yards in front of me, the tip of javelin coming my way. Just a dot in my field of vision, that had I not sidestepped would have impaled some part of my body. Which had the physique of, ironically, that javelin.

Basketball remained a passion that was seldom accompanied by great moves. Dad had built a plywood backboard on the flat-roofed, detached garage by the alley of the house and hung a rim so I could work on my 'skills.' When the ball bounced over the backboard and onto the roof, if you were quick enough you could run around the garage and catch the ball as it rolled off the other end. Which is only notable because two years later, that last turn around the corner would be the site of my first knee blowout.

High School Junior (Not a Good Year)

Oh, it started out okay, the usual school-and-related activities. October 18, 1969 was a Saturday and oddly, I was not out with friends. Instead, my father Pius and I had an unusually long chat that evening. I can still see those olive-green rockers with wooden arms where we sat together. Flashback: not that evening, but on another occasion, I heard Dad utter the only swear words I ever remember coming out of his mouth. We were working in the garage on something, don't remember what it was but I messed up and it was no doubt either costly and/or irreplaceable. Dad exclaimed, "Goddammit I try to show you how to do something and you f..k it up!" Tried to do everything just right for quite some time after that.

Back to Saturday night. After my long chat with Dad, I went to bed and was woken around 2 a.m. by my mother screaming for me. Brother Al was in the Navy at the time, stationed in California, so it was just the three of us. For the moment. Dad was having a heart attack, his second in as many years. In retrospect he was gone already, but Mom placed the nitroglycerin under his tongue and stayed in hysteria. 911 had been called. I could think of nothing to do other than go to the front door and furiously turn the outside light on and off repeatedly, so the emergency personnel could find the house more easily. Didn't matter. A couple of weeks shy of his 63rd birthday my hard-working, fun-loving, pied piper of kids was dead.

The next couple of weeks were a whirlwind of the depressing acts of putting him to rest. Al flying home. The traditional open casket viewing, rosaries, Catholic mass and finally, mercifully, burial. It's funny how the great ones stay with us. Eventually the pain of loss is dulled by the pleasant memories, which over time are magnified.

I see him in my boys, and my grandson. I think of him whenever I get a child to laugh, or fall asleep in my arms. Apparently one of his best qualities, a joyous love for the little ones, didn't fall too far from the tree. I'm thankful for that. And for the example he set.

I made the varsity basketball team that year, something Dad would have been proud of. Rode that pine, something he wouldn't have said much about. Mixing it up for rebounds against taller players was still fun, particularly when one was able to steal one away and hear the coach yell at the starter. To this day I rail on players' inability to make free throws, something my sons roll their eyes over. (The other is not hustling down the first base line in baseball). At the end of practice, we weren't allowed to shower until we made 20 of 25 free throws. Miss the sixth one and start over. Some guys took a LONG time to get to the showers.

We settled into our new normal. Mom mourning and carrying on with work. Al back in the Navy. And yours truly rebelling by discovering alcohol. For a time I didn't behave particularly well, something I do regret. I'll leave it at that.

High School Senior (A Newer Normal)

About six months before Dad passed away, a gentleman across the street and three doors down lost his wife to leukemia. Six months after his passing, Walter would begin a good old-fashioned courtship of my mother. Both had been married to their spouses for over 25 years, Mom and Dad for 27. Mom, 57 years old at the time, would tell Walter that she would not be seen out in public with another man for a full year after Dad's death. She owed him that much. So Walter complied, and pretty much every weekend would come over to the house with candy or flowers, and they would play cards. Pinochle mostly. After the obligatory year had passed, they began to go out to dinner together.

Walter was not my dad, and in my adolescent mind didn't measure up, but Mom was happier than I had seen her in some time. In retrospect he was a wonderful man who worshipped her and gave her a new lease on life. I came to appreciate him more and more over the years. In early 1971, as I was looking forward to graduation, Walter proposed to Mom. She did not say yes right away, rather telling him that she would first need the approval of her two boys. So she came to each of us and asked our opinion on the matter. Of course we said yes. That June, they were married. They would go on to a happy life together, Walter buying their dream home in north Bismarck, where they would stay until Walter passed away—31 years later. Which made them a very unusual couple, having both celebrated double silver wedding anniversaries, with their first spouses and then each other.

Walt and Sally would be the only grandparents on my side our two boys would ever know, with a larger generation gap (Dad was nearly 47 and Mom almost 41 when I was born) and Dad's early departure from this earth making paternal grandparents the stuff of tales gone fuzzy and relegated to much later ancestry research.

Senior Class President 'Slinky' Jahner

Not sure what possessed me to run for class president, but encouragement from friends didn't hurt. At first there were four of us running for the somewhat coveted, largely ceremonial post. Two were close friends, both of whom decided they didn't want the job and dropped out, pledging their support to me. So I was less the guy elected than the guy remaining after the other guy was not elected.

Along with the role came President of the student body. I was continually pressed by my constituents to lobby the school administration about such heady issues as relaxing the dress code to include jeans. That was a non-starter at a Catholic school in the fall of 1970.

The role turned out to be very good experience for a youngster. I read the announcements over the PA at the end of each school day. I presided over homecoming festivities, introducing speakers and acts, and on the evening of the bonfire/snake dance to the big game (we were trounced) I had the honor of lighting the bonfire. What I was not told was that some genius thought the requisite amount of gasoline to pour onto the stack of wood, cardboard and paper products was around 50 gallons. The blowback left me without eyebrows and lashes for a couple of months.

In a fairly inglorious weekend at the state wrestling championship in Minot I didn't do the office of the president any favors. After good friend Pat, from our rival high school, won the championship at his weight class, there were the obligatory post-match parties. In the act of walking down a hallway in a ("Why Not") Minot hotel where we were staying, I was grabbed by a nice man in blue and told "We're going to sober you up." Upon which I was, without benefit of a test, breathalyzer or phone call, escorted to the county jail (the city jail was full) to spend the evening with assorted felons. Of course, word found its way back to the school where I was welcomed with a couple of very uncomfortable chats with the superintendent and disciplinarian, followed by expulsion for two days with "double zeros" in all of my classes—which turned out to be a non-event since there were no tests on those two days and attendance wasn't graded. So no impact on graduating fifth in the class (don't get too excited; there were only 105 of us). However, it did lead to a creative line by one of our school newspaper writers, under a picture of me reading from notes to the school assembly. "Rod 'Slinky' Jahner. Let me present my case." (of beer, cute). The Slinky handle would take me three moves in two states and around five years to shake. Probably a bit prophetic with the comment. By graduation day the money we made on a class car wash, sale of services and other brainstorms was used to buy party supplies. Which included the four kegs that were sitting in the alley behind my house during the ceremony, thankfully unbeknownst to my mother. (See *behaved badly*, above.)

Shortly after graduation, as briefly alluded to in my sophomore year, I would blow out my first knee while shooting around in the backyard court. An injury that would be repaired now with a day surgery scoping followed by two days on crutches, required four days in the hospital in traction to unlock the knee, followed by major surgery, fourteen stitches and six weeks on crutches. Which is how I hopped into Walt and Sally's wedding in June, 1971.

Junior College Life

For some reason, probably not having the guts to do otherwise, I left high school as an honor student and proceeded to Bismarck Junior College with no idea of what I wanted to do with my life. It has remained one of my pet peeves, to this day, that schools do a mediocre job at best of going beyond teaching the basics. What was sorely needed in my day, and I sense to a large extent today as well, is useful career education juxtaposed with helping students explore alternatives and discover their passions. Teenagers often don't have a clue about these things, and I fit squarely into that mold at the time.

One thing I did discover is that drinking fairly heavily can easily drop a full point off of your grade point average. Went from a 3.8 overall in high school to 2.75 my first year of college. Thankfully the trend was reversed in the ensuing three years, but not before I successfully wrecked a couple of cars in the process. Really should have apologized to those people whose tree I took out after passing out and totaling my mother's Plymouth Fury in the process. I would wander close to a couple other near misses, and enumerate at least three occasions where I should have died behind the wheel of a car. Thankfully that didn't happen and nor did I hurt anyone else. Somehow, someone upstairs was watching out for me, and while I escaped relatively unscathed, I did cause my poor mother a considerable amount of grief at a time when she was least prepared for it. I remain sorry for that to this day, and admire the current generation, who when testing their limits, at least have the common sense to stay out of their cars more so than we did. Sure could have used Uber in those days.

There's nothing that special about waking up in a ditch going about 70 miles an hour. Laundry problem.

Summer and during-school jobs were eclectic. Choosing to stock grocery shelves at 4 a.m. three days a week for the extra 15 cents per hour over the regular-hours job was an interesting choice. Assisting in the delivery and installation of washers and dryers had its intriguing moments. Start with drilling a vent hole into a house under construction where the electricians had not turned off the outside power, resulting in the zipper of my parka touching/exploding/ melting as I leaned into it. To this day I don't remember how I relocated eight feet away from that spot in a nanosecond. Or the installation in a mobile home that had at least 100 cats in cages. The odor was such that we could work for about a minute at a time before going out for air. My stepfather Walter managed to get me summer jobs at the Highway Department, where one year I began by pulling weeds on the roadside all day, every day. That lasted about a week until I got to know the foreman and was placed on a tractor mowing for the rest of the summer. The following summer I drove the paint supply truck on a striping crew. It was actually kind of fun handling a twin axel, ten-speed behemoth. Spent my uneventful 21st birthday in Minot, North Dakota that summer, staying over on a striping run. Now back at the site of my high school incarceration, perhaps I should have looked up that nice officer to let him know I was now legal.

I always told my sons that they should have jobs IN their life that they don't want FOR their life. I lived that one by example to be sure. And they have. I've quite possibly bored them to tears with the stories. Sorry I'm not sorry boys, it's all on paper now.

College Life—UND

I followed my older brother's footsteps to the University of North Dakota in Grand Forks. Home of the Fighting Sioux. That is until, in recent years, NCAA political correctness took the name away, which means today they are the Fighting Hawks. Not for me. Hawks is a nice acronym for How About We Keep Sioux? I have the t-shirt to prove it. Personally, I believe the NCAA will be happy only when all college teams are named after fruit. Fighting Peaches anyone? That should strike fear into opponents. Ralph Englestad must be spinning in his grave. He was a goalie for the Sioux who went on to a very successful career and would build the $100 million hockey stadium for the school, on the condition that the Sioux name would remain. He then inserted that iconic Indian head logo everywhere in the stadium, and I mean everywhere. Thousands of them. Inlaid in the tile, etched in glass, carved into seat armrests, and more. When the name change was forced, the NCAA said that a 'reasonable' number of the logos would need to be removed. To take them all out, you would have to almost tear down the stadium.

The irony of the change is not lost on many. The Sioux logo was designed by a Native American. At the time when the Seminoles at Florida state kept their name (with a white guy in war paint, wielding a spear and riding around the stadium at games) there were more Native American teachers at UND than students at Florida state. In either case, what is offensive about the name of a tribe anyway?

Now, Savages and Redskins, those are offensive monikers. In North Dakota the population of one reservation voted overwhelmingly in favor of keeping the name, and the other abstained (thanks to an uncooperative tribal council member) which the NCAA deemed a big no. Please.

But I digress. I graduated from UND with a degree in mathematics, and minor in computer science. Oh, and with no earthly clue what I wanted to do with them. I did take with me my Frenchy's beer mug, personalized like hundreds of others and kept behind the bar at the establishment of the same name where I honed a reasonably good foosball game during my college years. I still have that mug. When Frenchy passed away a couple of years ago, I dusted it off and had a beer at our local watering hole in his honor.

There were a great collection of stories from college days, like most of us have. The better of these are reserved for the Gone....To A Better Life chapter of this work, where I honor, among others, two of my best friends and former roommates who left this world too soon.

For my part I went back to Bismarck to start my professional career rather unceremoniously. With a couple more jobs that I would have IN my life that I didn't want FOR my life. But someone upstairs continued to look out for me in that regard as well.

First Big-People Jobs

Social Services of the state of North Dakota in Bismarck paid $600 per month in 1975. Which was $25 less than the other offer I'd received, from a company that wanted me to run a computer on the graveyard shift. Such were the choices for a math major. My first tasks were to balance, by hand calculator, county-level detailed spreadsheets of various statistics. Which meant adding 53 rows and 12-14 columns down and across. It was mind-numbing work that left me, to this day, skilled at a ten-key calculator. That and about six bucks will get you a coffee. So, in today's terms, I earned around 3-4 cups of coffee per day. Which was about what I was drinking at the time, along with smoking 1.5 packs of menthol cigarettes each day. I was so wired that when someone walked up to my desk from behind and said hello, I threw my pencil into the ceiling. Decided it was time to quit smoking, which turned into a three-year ordeal, quitting cold turkey either on New Year's Eve or on Ash Wednesday, then starting right up again while sitting in a duck blind in the fall at around 100 degrees below zero. I finally chewed my way through a duck season and kicked cigarettes. It was easier to quit chewing tobacco than cigarettes. Not optimal, but effective. The opposite protocol was utilized by a brick-laying friend who was somewhat addicted to Copenhagen chewing tobacco, to the tune of 2-3 cans per day. He actually took up smoking for a time to stop chewing.

While at Social Services I discovered a report-writing software program that would do my mindless work for me. When I presented it to management, they thought I was the second coming. Mainframe-based and long before the advent of personal computers, the software was easy to program and made me look somewhat intelligent. On top of the world. Literally on top of the world, for I worked on the 17th floor of the state capital building, which at 18 stories was the tallest building in the entire state. By a bunch. I think my raise was another cup of coffee.

Second job was at Job Service, also in Bismarck, where I first documented every piece of Management Information (reports on top of reports) in an effort to simplify reporting across the organization. Which led to a job in the Research & Statistics Division, an interesting transition to the math behind employment services. The Job Service posts were secured for me by my lifelong friend, Glen's dad Alex. Alex could drink you under a table and keep you in stitches all night. Also a terrific manager and one of the better presenters I ever saw, naturally funny and informative. Something to aspire to.

One day the Executive Director asked me to do the same job he had just completed before his appointment by the governor: Run the re-election campaign of that governor, Art Link. The way he positioned it, I would need only to schedule his appearances, keep track of the funds, and remind him not to pick his neck when speaking. Not sure if he was entirely serious about that last one, but it stuck with me for some weird reason. Upon re-election, the governor would then gift me with an agency to run as a thank you. Just didn't sound like what I wanted to do, so I turned it down. There are tipping points in all of our lives and, in retrospect, this was the first major one for me. While at the time I thought I was giving up a cushy opportunity, there were other adventures in front of me. It worked out for the best anyway, as Governor Link narrowly lost that election in 1980 thanks to a variety of outside political forces that neither I nor anyone else could have overcome. So the 'getting your own agency' thing wasn't destined to be, anyway.

Golf in North Dakota

My brother introduced me to golf when I was in high school. He would groove that disgustingly natural swing while I would evolve into a bogey golfer (hacker), bottoming out later in life at a somewhat respectable 13 handicap. We have enjoyed a number of tourneys (and made a few bucks) at his club in Santa Fe, as well as visited St. Andrews together on a bucket list trip.

Most would not think of North Dakota as a golf destination. I have not played many of the great courses the state has to offer, but do have very fond memories of a few. Our season was at least six months long, some years longer. I started playing at Tom O'Leary, a hilly but wide-open track in Bismarck that was a great learning spot. (Also the site of the very steep #3 hole at the time, where I took my final toboggan ride). In spite of #3, I learned to love the game on that nine-hole course, which has since become eighteen.

The first course I loved was Riverwood. Aptly named as it was carved out of heavily wooded river bottoms. If you were off the fairway, you'd better be good at punching out through the trees, something I became good at since I missed a lot of fairways. There were days in the fall when the fog rolled in from the Missouri river in the early mornings (our favorite tee times) to the point that visibility was about 100 feet. Not a great thing for following a little white ball zooming away at nearly 100 miles per hour. So, we played with orange golf balls before they became fashionable to get a bead on the direction of the ball before the orange tracer disappeared into the mist. We seldom lost balls as we knew the course so well, and after a few holes the fog would burn off. Very cool.

Much later in life, after moving away, a course called Hawktree would be built in the hills north of Bismarck. I recommend it highly: at one point it made Golf Digest's public courses to play. The rolling hills are picturesque enough by themselves, but carve newly sodded fairways among the wispy prairie grass and you have the beginnings of a great golf experience. The other unique feature is the jet-black sand traps, utilizing ground up coal shale that plays very much like a fine sand. The contrast of colors is stunning and the course layout is varied and challenging. Wonderful place to play.

On a more recent trip, Al and I were taken to Bully Pulpit Golf Course in western North Dakota, ranked as one of America's 100 best public golf courses. Named after the Rough Rider, former North Dakota resident and former president Teddy Roosevelt, it is carved out of the Badlands. Half of the holes are in the lowlands and the other half straight up into the steep hills, offering unparalleled vistas and shots that rise, fall and go across the bluffs. Great experience.

Most people I meet say they have never met anyone from North Dakota. And those who endeavor to visit every state have often missed it. So, it stands to reason that most golfers won't know about the great playing opportunities there either. That's ok. We don't want too many of you up there anyway.

Chapter Three

→ Single Life in Denver

While at Job Service I was sent to Denver on a training course that involved cutting edge (at the time) management reporting. It was at this course that I met, and gravitated toward, two Department of Labor executives who were embarking on a federally funded project. Back in Bismarck I was approached by our Job Service Executive Director with an offer from them: Move to Denver, work part-time on their project while going to grad school at the University of Denver (today Daniels School of Business) for an MBA in Operations Research. The working team would include the university head of Operations Research, along with the two Department of Labor executives, and me. For my inconvenience, I would retain my full-time salary from Job Service, while the nice people from Labor would pay for the MBA. Not too difficult a decision. And by the way, thank you, taxpaying reader, for my education.

The project would utilize two databases from Job Service (North Dakota was chosen as the test state thanks to its reasonable size and my expertise there), one including all available applicants registered at Job Service, and the other the available jobs. Layered on those databases were all of the hiring constraints that Congress had laden upon the Job Service offices. These were rules that would ensure fair treatment by race, sex, handicap, nationality, veteran status, age, you get the idea. Some of the constraints were parity based (serve the same amount of one group as another) and others were percentage based (find jobs for x% of a given group). There were, count them, thirteen different constraints, all of which could be expressed mathematically. Incidentally, if a handicapped female Vietnam-era veteran of color would have walked into a Job Service office, a motherload of constraints would have been hit simultaneously. If there wasn't a job for her in the database, they would've hired her on the spot.

So now we have (1) people, (2) jobs and (3) constraints on the pairings of (1) and (2). The vision was that this could be turned into a giant linear programming model. For those of you who are not math nerds, this was an optimization technique we would use to calculate the best overall solution for the Job Service offices to meet all of the requirements placed on them. The working hypothesis was that there was so much complexity that there would not be a solution. All the while, congressmen and women were being re-elected in part because of the wonderful things they were doing from Washington for special interest groups.

We spent over a year working on algorithms that matched all of the jobs to potential applicants on file. So now we had the makings of a mathematical problem, albeit a big one. The head of Operations Research programmed the problem, submitted it to the computer, and the problem was too large for the University of Denver's mainframe. Four people had spent a year and a half working on a problem created by government regulations that had no possibility of being solved in one of the smallest sample sizes in the land. Our government in action. Sadly, I didn't hold onto the paper I wrote about the project, so it's now keeping mom's high school paper company somewhere.

After the project, and with my MBA studies completed, there was a federal hiring freeze, so I was sent on my way. Can't make this stuff up.

Joining Stuff in Denver

Denver was a great place to cut my teeth on city life, which I began doing soon after I arrived. Lots of outdoor and sporting opportunities. No, I wasn't much of a skier, North Dakota being perhaps the flattest state in the country. First question asked in Colorado (before "Where do you ski?") is always "Where are you from?"—since most are transplants. You get funny looks when your answer is North Dakota, but on the upside, I didn't button a coat for the first two years I lived there. Compared to North Dakota, Colorado was balmy.

I joined stuff. A couple of softball teams and intramural basketball at DU for starters. Then I discovered coed sports, including volleyball, softball and bowling. A great way to meet people. Coed bowling, now that's a rough sport. I had bowled in leagues back home so it was a good fit. No pressure but there was considerable entertainment. On one of my first trips to an alley, I witnessed a gentleman with his girlfriend. She was about 21 years old, with a body that didn't stop until next Tuesday and a blouse that was unbuttoned to her waist. He was at least 50, a bit portly, loaded with gold chains and a shirt that was, sadly, also unbuttoned to the waist. I watched in amusement as he taught her the "classic" three-step delivery, which I had never seen before. There is a reason for that. It's worthless. We happened to exit at the same time they were leaving in his Caddy, around the size of a small condo, with a personalized license plate that said OK DUDE. Wow, just Wow.

The coed softball league—The Up-the-Creek Softball Association—was a gas. Around 70 teams playing all over southeast Denver on Sunday mornings. Guys batted opposite hand as an equalizer. In the afternoon after the games, Coors was nice enough to park a semi full of kegs (free of charge to us) at Garland Park, where volleyball nets, frisbees and thirst emerged. So did long days at work on Mondays.

One of my men's softball teams played in two different leagues, with two different sponsors: the first was a local watering hole named the Bull & Bush that is still there today, the other a printing company who chose jerseys with an array of bright orange stripes from the middle down, ala the old Houston Astros. We played a little different caliber ball than the A's. We did have a reasonably good team, and the leagues had skill rankings ranging from 'Competitive' to A, B, C and D. We played at the 'A' level, one step from the top. Feeling good about ourselves, we joined a Competitive tournament one weekend, just for grins. We lost the first game 24-2 and it wasn't that close. Those guys broke two windshields in the parking lot outside of the stadium. The guttural grunts that resonated from their dugout when the moonshots left their bats were something other than human. We returned to our 'A' roots from that day on.

The Bull & Bush would eventually become the site of my bachelor party, where among other shenanigans, the female pimp of a male prostitute propositioned one of my ushers. You might need to re-read that a couple of times. While usher Tim, a.k.a. 'Rat,' was a 'cute guy,' he did not escape the occasional (well, more than occasional) taunts for the rest of the evening and beyond.

All in all I had a great time joining stuff, managed to stay in good shape, and meet many good friends. One of whom would become my wife.

Meeting Cindy

Along with a friend, Phil, whom I'd met shortly after moving to Denver, I decided to attend a rather large ski club party. I wasn't in a club yet, as I had yet to try the sport. Seemed a bit silly to drive a couple of hours to where everyone else was going for recreation. Back home, we drove to get away from people, and there weren't that many to start with. But I digress.

The party was as expected, crowded, and had a very good band. To get a beer one needed to wade through patrons that were three-deep at the bar. So, we started a routine of taking turns getting two beers for each other when needed.

I met some of my softball buddies and there were a number of girls with them. My shortstop and team captain introduced me to Cindy Hill, whereupon this exchange occurred:

Me: "Hi, I'm Rod, how do you like me so far?"
Cindy: "Not much. Where are you from?"
Me: "North Dakota."
Cindy: "No one is from North Dakota. What sign are you?" This one dripping with sarcasm.

Me: "Stop."

As if on cue, Phil wandered by and handed me a beer on his way back to see a group he had met. Cindy looked a bit puzzled and asked, "Do you have people for that?"

I would find out later that my team captain wanted to date Cindy, but we clicked from the start and that was that. Which gave me pause when considering what would happen to my playing time. Thankfully, he was not that shallow.

The first time Cindy saw my car, a snappy little red Toyota Corolla SR5, she asked why there was an electrical plug protruding from the engine compartment. When I told her that's how we start our cars in North Dakota in the winter, she looked at me like I had three heads. (I've seen that look a few times since.)

And so it began, sparring from the start, discovering we had the same cutting sense of humor, continuing to this day. We would eventually create two boys who had no chance at being normal.

I love it when a plan comes together.

Almost forgot, I'm making this sound like we have a forever thing. Actually, there's an (unwritten) 40-year contract. As of the beginnings of this writing we were at 39, so in May of 2022 she completed her option year. More on how that worked out later.

Never stops being funny, does it, dear?

First Date

Shortly after meeting I asked Cindy over to my condo in southeast Denver for dinner. Wish I could remember what I cooked for her. What we both remember were the epic frozen Brandy Alexanders I made. (Just talked to her and she can't remember the meal either. "After your Brandy Alexanders how do you expect me to remember dinner?")

What I do recall, very clearly, was the immediate connection. We had dinner, I made a blender of those Alexanders, and we sat on the small balcony of my condo talking for hours and hours. From similarities (both losing our dads way too early, she at 11, me at 17), to differences (North Dakota and Ohio were just a bit eclectic), the common ground, early-on, was our ability to make each other laugh. It was Just. So. Comfortable. A part of me knew that night that I had found my soulmate, but it took a while for me to pull the trigger.

I 'proposed' on Christmas Eve, 18 months after we met, an evening she to this day ridicules me for (and for good reason). First of all, that friendship ring I gave her was taken way differently than I anticipated. The next thing I knew she was planning a wedding. One of these days I'll actually ask her to marry me. Secondly, I had (not so smartly) planned a trip back to North Dakota to see Mom so I left the next day. Not my finest hour but she has since publicly exacted the appropriate pound of flesh.

Before we were allowed to be married in the Catholic Church, we went through a certified marriage encounter experience, this particular one at a weekend retreat in the Rocky Mountains just outside of Denver. There were a number of class topics on life skills, interpersonal relationships, etc., and a personal assignment where we were asked to write each other a love letter. I kept that bit of prose for some time and thought including it here might be the best tribute to Cindy. Written while relaxing by a little river in the mountains, it was titled "Down By The Old

Mill Stream." Sadly, it somehow found the same fate as my mother's paper about the family immigration through the eyes of her father—lost. In the search process, I did find two handwritten notes, an exercise we were asked to do at the time. We were to list our expectations of our life together, and to prioritize the top five. The lists, written independently 40 years ago, were quite compatible, to say the least:

1. Cindy: Being happy with each other as we are today.
   Rod: Trust

2. Cindy: Being supportive of each other.
   Rod: Complete honesty/conflicts to be solved diplomatically.

3. Cindy: Having two kids, Drew & Sasha.
   Rod: Children, two if possible.
   (Mission accomplished, though two boys and the names didn't stick).

4. Cindy: Someday moving to a new town together/having Rod get transferred abroad.
   Rod: Having the dominant career and therefore most likely relocating.
   (Transfer to Singapore covered this one nicely)

5. Cindy: Having time to enjoy it all.
   Rod: Time for myself/give Cindy the same.

After the mountain retreat, we also had multiple sessions of counseling with a wonderful, successfully married couple. Homework between sessions, valuable conversations, introspection, the works. While we were a little older than most of the intended couples of the time (both 28), we did find the experience very useful, and I recommend this sort of exercise for anyone to this day. On the last of our sessions at the consulting couple's home, the priest who would marry us visited. At the end of that session, he asked if we had any questions. (Sidebar, a few years before that time, the Church had decided to eliminate the recognition of 'Limbo', which was a special place in heaven for infants who passed away before being baptized to remove Original Sin from their souls, as Catholics believe.) I asked the good Father, "So the Church closed Limbo. Where did all those little babies go?" This poor man looked at me like I had lost my mind. As God is my witness, he left the priesthood a couple of weeks after we were married. I always wondered if I was in some small way his tipping point....

More Dating in Denver

Cindy and I had a great time getting to know each other. Much of the time revolved around sports, playing softball, attending movies, or going to the occasional Broncos game. Tough tickets to land in those days. The season ticket waiting list was 20+ years long, so you needed to find a really good friend. Case in point, Cindy relayed stories of Bronco's tickets being divided as a part of divorce settlements. Apparently not an uncommon occurrence which created some uncomfortable cheering moments.

We liked a lot of the same things, which is handy. So, one holiday evening Cindy decided to treat me to a bit of culture. Handel's Messiah. Not exactly my cup of tea but she was excited. During intermission I ordered a beer and the woman behind the counter looked at me as if I had spat on the counter. I heard another woman exclaim with her hand pasted to her forehead, "Oh the pace is just killing." Personally, I thought it was going a little slow. Afterwards this was our exchange:

Cindy: "How did you like it?"

I then recited the number of men and women in the choir, and the number of each instrument in the orchestra, and continued "At the end I was working on the male/female split of each instrument."

Cindy: "Didn't like it, did you?"

Rod: "No."

Ok, I've grown a (little) bit since. Back then, you could take the boy out of North Dakota, but.....

At this time Cindy was working at an office furniture company, Kissler Quill, as a buyer. She answered her phone "Cindy Hill of Kissler Quill." Darling. She would later move to Public Service Company of Colorado in a similar position. Hers was often a job where she had to say no to executives who wanted furniture or equipment that was above their pay grade. While she was there, we were married, and after she became Cindy Jahner, one of her in-house customers happened to call. He was pleased with her service to the point that he exclaimed that she was "so much nicer than that bitch Cindy Hill." Whereupon she took delight in letting him know that they were one and the same.

The group of common friends we had from the start grew over time, and many, including me, had August birthdays. So many that there was soon an annual August Birthdays Party. Sadly, we placed second in the egg toss championship at the last of those parties.

Inappropriate Dietary Selections

The third baseman on one of my softball teams had a unique habit of drinking beer out of shoes. Sometimes other people's shoes. After a game. The cleats that had been worn in the game. After one particular post game, it became hard to forget watching our waitress balancing a softball cleat full of beer on her tray as she delivered it to him. The 'tradition' continued throughout a couple of seasons and into our wedding, where he led a shoe toast participated in by every guy in attendance, including my boss who was a VP at Citibank at the time.

There were a number of guys from Pennsylvania on that team so there was more than our share of Rolling Rock (The Green Death) consumed after practices. Which tasted to me not unlike a beer out of a shoe. (Yeah, I had a few from a shoe, myself).

Fast-forward about a quarter of a century where eldest son Kyle scores his first 'try' playing club rugby for the USC Trojans. At the post-game party he is therefore required to 'shoot the boot,'—drink a beer out of his shoe. Which he does. A fraternity brother notices him using both hands, however, a clear breach of protocol, as leaving the right-hand condensation-free when having cocktails is necessary to allow for shaking hands with new acquaintances, and says, "I think I saw a little right hand there, so you're going to have to do that again." Kyle's second shoe beer was done correctly, left hand only. Fast-forward to Kyle's wedding and you guessed it, a shoe-drinking ceremony at the reception. Bride-approved.

Family traditions kind of bring a tear to your eye, don't they?

Now let's talk flowers. Shortly after I graduated college, a friend attended a wedding where the guys in the wedding party thought it cute to have a ceremony honoring the new couple where they ate their boutonnieres. Then they escalated to the bride and groom's wedding table, where they leveled the daisy centerpiece. Not sure what food was served at that wedding but it was clearly inadequate. And so it began, following that fateful night, with every wedding amongst our circle of friends having a groomsman flower-eating ceremony. Over the years I became something of a connoisseur of carnations, learning what colors were more tasty or bitter than others. I was partial to white and the pastels, and frowned upon the orange and red ones. Blue just plain frightened me for some reason.

When it came time for Cindy and me to plan our wedding, you might be stunned to learn this was the topic of our first fight. Her mother had chosen handmade artificial bouquets for her bridesmaids, and wanted matching artificial flowers on the groomsman's lapels. I said no. She asked why. I replied, "I've eaten a flower at every one of these clowns' weddings, and they're going to eat one at mine." This went back and forth until she finally relented. And got her own revenge. While my boys had carnations, she had me wear a rose. THAT was a challenge. Made me long for a blue carnation.

Alaska, Appendix, Raisins and Jack

Brother Al had a job in Juneau, Alaska for a number of years, as cash manager for the state government. So it afforded me the opportunity to travel there on vacation a few years running in the early 80's. Fishing in the Salmon Derby was a terrific time. Halibut fishing is a gas also. Like pulling a rock up through 120 feet of water, only to have him see light and dive straight back down. On my first trip to Juneau one guy fishing by himself had landed a 300 pound halibut with a sport rod, using 75 pound test line. Apparently took him over three hours to haul it in, and when the $1000 fish was finally beside the boat he had no choice but to shoot it, gaff it and tow the prize back to the dock.

Side trips to places like Glacier Bay and Skagway were great, scenic fun. One year Al arranged a getaway to an isolated forest service cabin for a few days of fishing. He, Fast Eddie (rest his soul) and I boarded a float plane which dropped us off at the lake, a good hundred miles from nowhere. The cabin was small and comfortable, with an outside cupboard for food that might attract bears in case they decided to wander through. Canned goods could be kept inside.

On our second day there, another float plane happened to fly over, and tilted his wings back and forth when we waved. Which got us thinking: *We are in the middle of nowhere*. No mobile phones yet, no communications ability whatsoever and the next time we would see anyone was when our own plane retrieved us in three more days. Surrounded by forest at this little lake, should someone get sick we would have a problem. The topic of appendicitis came up, as one possibility that can happen anytime and require immediate attention. Our plan, should there be an emergency, was to take what little fuel there was available, light the cabin on fire and stand in the water waiting for someone to notice the smoke. Two weeks to the day after we had that conversation, Al's appendix ruptured, requiring not one but two emergency surgeries in Juneau. Had that happened out in the bush, there would not have been enough time to save him. Guess it wasn't his time.

Turned out to be colder than expected on that trip in August, and we didn't have coffee cups. We did, however, have beer cans, which we cut the tops off of, and filled with a delectable mixture of heated Tang (orange-flavored drink mix originally developed for astronauts) and our friend Jim Beam. Gloves required to hold the beer cans full of this hot 'wonderfulness.' Seemed like the thing to do at the time.

When our float plane picked us up for the trip back, we flew over and through mountains and at one point the pilot banked severely to give us a great view of an albino deer laying in the snow. I took what I thought were going to be great pictures, but did I mention albino deer in snow? So I ended up with really nice pictures of....snow.

They partied for distance in Juneau. Alaska has the highest per capita alcoholism rate of any state, isolation certainly a contributor. One year I attended the annual Save The Raisins Party. The previous year's party involved participants climbing to the top of Mt. Robert, overlooking Juneau, changing into formal attire and listening to a baby grand piano (helicoptered in, of course) while imbibing and enjoying the spectacular vistas and view of the city below. The party I attended was at a mystery location, with the dress code requiring all to wear a flower. Dogs included.

We met and were bussed around the area for a while before stopping at the party site, a trucking warehouse. One loading dock was the bar for everyone's favorite beverages, another had movies of the previous Raisins party atop Mt. Robert, and a third housed the band. Great time. I asked more than one participant, "Why Raisins?" The only response I ever received was "Why Not?"

The following year, my old friend Mike from Bismarck, who was working in Anchorage at the time, came down to Juneau to meet me on my annual excursion. We stopped into a local watering hole on Douglas Island, whereupon the bartender took one look at us and asked, "You guys aren't from around here, are you?" Before we had said no and because he knew the answer to his own question, he turned around, poured two shots and placed them in front of us, commanding us to "drink those." We poured them down, and he continued, "That was Jack. Welcome to Alaska." Some (well, maybe one) of you might think he was conjuring the spirit of Alaska's most famous writer, Jack London. I can assure you, no. He was referring to Mr. Daniels.

One Titanic to Another

When my job with the Department of Labor ended, and with my newly-minted MBA in hand (thank you again, fellow taxpayers), a friend from Denver University told me about a financial analyst position with Citibank in Denver. I interviewed, landed the job and began what would turn out to be a 23-year journey from Colorado to Missouri to Singapore.

Didn't see that coming.

Six weeks into the job at a first ever, draft-driven ready-credit business, the business CEO was standing at my desk on a Friday afternoon, visibly shaken and informing me of the credit and collections problem that existed in what would turn out to be the first of more than one interesting landing spots for me at the bank. On Monday morning I would be assigned to a four-person team whose project was to revamp the collections department, as the business was blowing up.[1] Seems that someone misread some credit bureau information on a grand scale and gave a bunch of unemployed folks nice big loans that they quickly maxed out and weren't repaying. I couldn't spell Collections without a six-letter head start at that time. Which was ironic since the CEO couldn't spell Credit without a four-letter head start.

We successfully completed the project, a learning experience indeed, and the portfolio continued to deteriorate. These were collectors, not magicians. Over the next couple of years, the staff of 200+ fell to under 100, the VPs had all left the burning ship and we had a new CEO. Those of us who were left occupied the corner offices. Nice digs with mahogany furniture, couch, love seat and 12th story view of the front range of the Rockies. I had become the Financial Controller, thanks in part to the advice of a boss who had become a good friend (rest his soul, he is honored later in these pages). His wise counsel had been to the effect that when the CEO interviewed me for the job

---

[1] "A blow up [or blowup] is a slang term used to describe the complete and abject failure of an individual, corporation, bank, development project, hedge fund, etc." – investopedia.com. I now have a footnote in this book. It's officially an official book.

and asked, "How much is two plus two?", the appropriate answer would be "How much do you want it to be?"

About six months later, one of the seniors from St. Louis who ran the business came out and gave us all a motivational speech, telling us that there would be no more cuts, and this was the group that the bank would go forward with. All the while he was resting his chin in his hand and looking at the ceiling. We went from that meeting directly to the copiers and started running off our résumés.

Before the place was folded up and moved to another entity, my friend Beth (now elevated to new CEO) and I were tiring of lying to our people about the 'positive state of the business.' So we went to a little Mexican restaurant in Southeast Denver, ordered lunch and a pitcher of Margaritas. And then another pitcher. And a third. When I arrived home Cindy took one look at me and said, "You're drunk," to which I replied "Yes, I am." The downside is that Beth and I were sitting on an outside deck as the sun set, and should have changed places on occasion. I was sunburned on one side of my face, she on the other. With our brown hair we looked like a pair of Neapolitan ice cream cones.

My next job at Citibank would be at a cobranded credit card business. My corner office was replaced with a first-floor table I shared with another analyst, and included an unobstructed view of the air conditioning unit outside. It was at that moment I realized you don't get too excited about your office in this company. This business took longer than six weeks to be in trouble. Six months. Seems that the operations side wasn't built quite right from the start.

Next stop, a relocation to St. Louis, much larger entity with national presence, and stability. Citimortgage. Which inside of three years blew up, sky high. The First Mortgage debacle of all debacles, caused by a marketing program that was flawed from the start and brought people to our doors who couldn't get a loan anywhere else. Final tab on that one, estimates as high as $3 billion.

Years later, when I moved into training, I would introduce myself to my audience telling them of my first three businesses in the bank, and that with my track record they should be concerned about being in the same room with me.

They say you learn a lot more by working through problems. I must be a genius.

Meeting The Fam

When Cindy and I had been dating for a year, she wanted me to see where she grew up and to meet her family. I had already met sister Lesley and brother-in-law Joe, who today thankfully live nearby and with whom we remain close. They all grew up in Mt. Vernon, Ohio, a bedroom community 50 miles northeast of Columbus. We made the trip over Thanksgiving, 1981. After the trip was arranged, Lesley informed Cindy, and then me, that her mother Madeleine had planned an engagement party to include around a hundred of her favorite friends. Which was interesting because I had not proposed. How do you define uncomfortable? After some objection from Cindy, the party was to go on.

On the day of the party, Joe picked me up for a morning workout, then an afternoon at Sir James, a local watering hole. We got along famously from the start, and were in a bit of trouble from the start as well. When dropped off back at the house less than an hour before the cocktail party in honor of my non-existent engagement, I was ushered upstairs to quickly clean up and change, and Joe returned to his parent's home to do the same.

In time for the gala, Joe and Lesley arrived just as I was coming downstairs. He was dressed stylishly for the time (as always) in a grey Harris tweed sport coat, black dress slacks, black shoes with matching belt, black conservative tie and a powder blue button-down shirt. I was dressed in a (copy and paste here) grey Harris tweed sport coat, black dress slacks, black shoes with matching belt, black conservative tie and (the sole departure) a white button-down shirt. We looked like we dressed together, something we have repeatedly and accidentally done many times over the years since. Can't count the number of times anymore, but it's a bunch, to the point of becoming a running joke between Cindy and I, "I wonder what Joe is wearing today."

This one gets better. Cindy's second stepfather (her father had passed away when she was 11 and the first stepfather died when she was 17) now descended the staircase wearing, you guessed it, a grey Harris tweed sport coat. Except that, rest his soul, he did not possess the sense of style that the other two matching boys did. He had completed his ensemble with a pair of Hilton Head bold green and blue plaid slacks. The only thing the outfit needed was floppy shoes and a red nose. He was quickly ushered back to change by Cindy's mom, Madeleine.

At five minutes to six, Madeleine announced that we should proceed to the front door as people would be arriving soon. Sure enough, at 6 p.m. sharp it started, and within

15 minutes the entire group was in the house. It was like you placed a drop of water on the floor and a party instantaneously sprang up. Over the next couple of hours I met some wonderful people. One was Del, Cindy's natural father's friend. Del regaled us with the story of his wedding day, when he and his new bride were leaving the church and he pushed her into the bushes. She asked, "What was that for?" His response, "That's for nothing, now stay in line." The story was bull, we both knew it, but it didn't stop us from breaking up in laughter. It was Del's way of making me comfortable in an uncomfortable setting.

At ten to eight, everyone started for the door, and they were all gone by 8 p.m. I was just getting into the party mood and as quickly as it had started, it was over. When Madeleine sent an invitation to a cocktail party from 6-8 p.m., by God it was going to be from 6-8 p.m. As I would find out later, they all no doubt had an 8 p.m. party somewhere else, anyway. At future events in years ahead, I would often be the designated bartender at these events, which was always great fun with this wonderful group of Cindy's family and friends.

Permanent Guest?

The first night I stayed at Cindy's family home was interesting, to say the least. With a double-story four post façade on the front, and an entry that greets you with a wood floor, chiming grandfather clock and sweeping cherry wood staircase with upstairs overlook, the lovely home had a majesty that somehow instantly reminded me of some of the scarier movies I'd seen in my life. It seemed the perfect setting for the stories Cindy had primed me with of her first stepfather, Tom. He had passed away in a car accident and apparently never really left the house that he loved. I'll leave justification for the claim of his ongoing presence in the house to Cindy, but suffice to say the stories were convincing, and did not sound the least bit crackpot. I was a believer.

When everyone else had retired to their rooms, I was in the upstairs bathroom taking out my contact lenses. Whereupon the bathroom door opened itself. No one was there. I could hear it behind me sweeping across the plush carpet. Just a bit disconcerting.

Two choices here. Create a new door through the wall of the second-floor bathroom (three stories in the back of the house), or investigate. I closed the door, not latching it, and waited. Thank God, it opened again to my realization that it was a bit out of plumb. A natural phenomenon that, for a moment, had manifested itself as *GET OUT*.

I finished pulling out my contacts, put on clean underwear, and went to bed.

Chapter Four

> → Family Life in St. Louis

The initial idea of moving from Denver, where Cindy and I had met, fallen in love, gotten married and were now awaiting our first son, was not exactly received with enthusiasm. I believe her exact words were "We'll miss you."

The interview—with another subsidiary of Citibank—was pushed back until Kyle was born. I flew out and upon return to Cindy's hospital bed told her we were moving. Pretty much the same enthusiasm followed. But move we did. It wouldn't be the only job change or relocation with the organization—where frequent evolutions of priorities, business successes and yes, failures—either presented unique opportunities or forced one to make a career change. Through the hard times I was loyal to a fault, and would ultimately stay for 23 years.

Initially commuting back and forth between Denver and St. Louis for a time, I soon found a new house for us and we sold our starter home in Denver. First-born parents traveling with a newborn terrified us, but it needn't have. When we pulled out of the driveway in Denver, Kyle, now a couple of months old, fell asleep. He slept through the drive to the airport, transfer to his carrier, onto the plane, through the flight, into the car seat in the rental car and to the hotel. He woke up in the hotel parking lot, blissfully unaware of any change in geography. Child from God. (Then we had Corey.)

All new houses have their own sounds to get used to. This one, in the suburbs, had some mileage on it (and the ugliest wallpaper on the planet), and was two stories in the front, three in the back with a basement walkout. The first night in bed, Cindy woke me and was certain there was someone downstairs. Just what I wanted to hear. So I went down, she following me. I cleared the first floor (all three rooms). Only possibility left was now the unfinished basement. I stood at the head of the stairs, not crazy about this situation and came up with an idea. I asked Cindy, standing right behind me, in a voice loud enough to be heard downstairs, "Where's my shotgun?" She replied, also in a voice that could be heard downstairs, "It's downstairs." To which I replied, "Great, now he's armed too." Turns out there was no one there, but the search process was, in a word, uncomfortable.

Not long after that day we awoke early one morning to the sound of a tornado siren. I took a glance outside and the sky did look a bit eerie. So we got up, woke the baby and headed for the (thankfully again unoccupied) basement. We stood there looking at a bewildered baby—who was not all that thrilled about leaving his REM sleep upstairs—for a good half hour. Nothing. Siren still blaring. Sky still clouded over but looking less threatening. I finally tired of the 'do you really have any idea what you are doing' looks on Cindy and Kyle's faces and ventured upstairs to investigate, only to realize that the tornado siren was in fact a car alarm. Later we would make the mistake of telling our new neighbors the story. They were more than amused.

Better days were ahead. St. Louis turned out to be a great family-oriented city that seemed more like a big town to us: For one thing, many natives had stayed. One of the first questions asked in casual conversation was, and I am not making this up, "What high school did you go to?"

My reply was always, "St. Mary's" which, as it turned out, was a fairly upscale school in St. Louis. When I heard the inevitable follow up questions, I told them, "No, St. Mary's Central High School in Bismarck, North Dakota." For some reason most people became less impressed at that point.

We lived there for thirteen years. Became rabid Cardinals baseball fans. Enjoyed a good number of games with our boys at Busch stadium, often followed by declaring a bad parent day on the way home, stopping at Ted Drew's for a dinner of giant frozen custards. The boys grew up playing every sport they could get their hands on. Starting with herd ball (beginner soccer, with a herd of boys around a ball that would eventually pop out and be followed by them all) and progressing to baseball, swimming, diving, basketball, street hockey, et al. And we met our network of friends, good ones, largely through watching with parents of other athletes. Idyllic in retrospect.

Weird Memory

When we moved to St. Louis, I visited the local DMV for a new driver's license. Nothing abnormal about the process until I was assigned a sixteen-digit number for my license.

I asked the woman behind the counter where they sourced that number, and she said it's just a number we assign to you. I said, "That's the same 16 digit number I had two states and over five years ago in North Dakota." J012-8000-6757-1516. She said I was crazy. I went home with this off the charts probability story and told Cindy that it was the same number. She said I was crazy. Not for the first time by the way.

Undeterred, the next time I was in North Dakota, I relayed my number story to a cousin who spent his career at the state Highway Department. He said there was a time when North Dakota and Missouri shared the algorithm for assigning driver's license numbers, jumbling personal data that never changes. So it made perfect sense that I would have been assigned the same number across that period. That said, he joined the ranks of those thinking me a bit loony, for being the one person he ever knew of who would have (a) lived in the two states at the times when those algorithms matched, and (b) be weird enough to have remembered the number five years later.

In point of fact, when in North Dakota as a teenager, I had grown tired of having to pull out my wallet every time an application required a driver's license number so I had committed it to memory. And it stuck. Hard. To this day. If I could get it out of my brain, perhaps I could remember something important for a change. That theory that we only utilize a fraction of our brain power? For me it goes the other way. I think I'm operating pretty much at full tilt all the time.

There is other weirdness in my head, but quite frankly you've heard all you need to for the moment.

Big and Bigger

Only parents can understand what becoming a parent does to your outlook on life. I'm no different. While I worked at not making this book a brag fest on our boys (something that I am want to do regularly), the pride for both was immediate and lasting.

Kyle was born a strapping 9 pounds even, which of course had me hitching up my pants and saying "Yeeeaaaah, that's my boy." Mom had sent a newborn outfit for him to wear from the hospital to our home, and the buttons were pilling on the thing as soon as we stuffed him into it. Worn once and put in a drawer.

Sidebar: The only newborn class we missed before his birth, thanks to a snowstorm in Denver, was on C-Sections. You guessed it, that's how he was born. Cindy, on local anesthesia and with me at her side, implored me: "Don't faint."

The anesthesiologist then added, "You faint, you'll stay on the floor and we'll walk over you." Fair enough. When Kyle didn't cry after emerging, Cindy was frightened. This prompted the good doctor to hold him up by the chest, facing Cindy, move Kyle's arms around and in his best ventriloquist act exclaim, "Hi Mommy."

Then along came Corey, weighing in at 10 pounds, 10 ounces. Cindy was not impressed with this trend. Dad and operating room nurses in a pool to guess the weight. One of the nurses said, "I've never bet on one this big!" A day later, onlookers at the nursery would exclaim, "Look, that poor baby was left behind," thinking he had been there way past his welcome. Proud dad again. When I called my mom with the news, the following exchange occurred:

Mom: "Which one of you does he look like?"

Rod: "Winston Churchill."

Mom: "Come on Rod, who does he look like?"

Rod: "Mom. He's 10-10. He has three chins. Put a cigar in his mouth and he's a dead ringer for Winnie."

I thought it was a good line.

Mom, not so much.

Boys—Early Years

Corey arrived just two years after Kyle. It was clear from the start there were a few differences. Kyle had been an easy child to rear, always happy. He ate anything put in front of him, and I can still see him take a handful of peas, put the entire hand into his mouth and unfurl it, not missing one pea. Corey's personality was a bit more demanding. Clue one, Cindy bought a book on raising the strong-willed child when he was six months old. A purchase that turned out to be quite prophetic.

The boys' love of sports was evident from very early on. Both were fanatical about playing everything. And spectating.

As young as six years old Kyle would happily curl up on the couch with me to watch football games, two in a day if I allowed it (which I did not). He was a savant of the NFL, able to draw, free hand, each helmet in the league from memory. In the fifth grade, a year-long geography assignment would be converted into "The NFL Teams and Their Cities." It filled a three-inch binder with Cindy learning more about the topics than she ever anticipated, serving as Kyle's typist. Over time he would turn out to be the hardest worker on the field with any team he joined. Not blessed with the natural ability of his younger brother, he would make himself into an athlete over time through sheer determination. He always wanted the difficult and visible job, goalie in soccer, catcher in baseball, tight end and center linebacker in football.

Corey was a natural. Anything with a ball, he could play. It started with soccer. While Kyle was waiting his turn for drills at his team practice, Corey had nothing to do but dribble a soccer ball on the sideline for hours. When he finally aged into a pre-kindergarten YMCA league, he scored 22 of the team's 24 goals in his first year. All that dribbling paid off.

Both would play outdoor and indoor soccer, as well as little league baseball, through their fifth and sixth grades (when we moved overseas). Sibling rivalry was always evident, as with most boys close in age. Corey would show his true colors with such shenanigans (a favorite word later in life) as patiently lying-in wait under Kyle's bed while he showered and upon returning to his bedside, reach out and grab his ankles. "He screamed like a little girl." After Kyle discovered a proficiency at weightlifting, those little pranks occurred less frequently.

Both were very good students, with Kyle taking the lead in this category. He was the quintessential student that teachers loved. Math in particular was a proficiency from an early age. When he was two I occasionally walked around the neighborhood with him riding on my shoulders playing numbers games. When we returned from one of our outings, he surprised his mother by counting to 100. One day at lunch with a five year-old Kyle, we suggested that

Corey had done something wrong and his mother and I were grounding him for two years. Kyle asked, "How many days is that?" I asked him to figure it out in his head, and about 30 seconds later he announced, "Seven-hundred and thirty."

"How did you do that?" I asked.

"Well, there are three-hundred and sixty-five days in a year, so I added the two three-hundreds for six-hundred, then put aside the fifteens from the sixty-fives and added the two fifties for another hundred. Fifteen and fifteen equals thirty, so, seven-hundred and thirty." And so it was, with us playing numbers games quite a lot.

When Corey was in kindergarten for his first day, the teacher left the room for a minute only to find him reading the blackboard to the class upon her return. She went to the principal and asked that he be tested, as she felt a bit silly starting "A" week with a kid who could already read, as it turned out, at a third-grade level. Guess reading all of those nighttime stories had paid off. So, he was promoted to first grade immediately, placing him one year behind his older brother in school. He asked us, since he was reading at a third-grade level, why he wasn't promoted to third grade. In grade school, Corey was not one to put in the hours that his older brother had made a habit. He still received very good grades, but would have teachers lamenting that he's not like Kyle. Which was irritating to us. We sort of liked the idea that they were different, and the school should not have expected otherwise.

Merry Christmas

Each and every year at Christmastime, I would drag my family to Alton, Illinois from St. Louis to cut down a tree for the holidays. Thirty-minute or so drive to a farm where they had a horse-drawn hayride out to the cutting area, saws provided, pick your own tree and play Daniel Boone. If the kids were lucky, they were invited to ride up front with the driver. After the cutting, the business bundled the tree and attached it to the top of the minivan for the ride home while we shopped in the little novelty store and drank hot chocolate. Never mind that Cindy and Corey had minor allergies to pine, the cold should cover that. Total cost of the tree, $22, versus the $75 plus at a tree lot in the city which had inferior products by comparison. Well worth the effort in my mind, if not my family's.

On one of these normal years we drove back to town with our new (large) tree tied to the top of the minivan. As we drove past our church, it occurred to me that if we hurried home to change, we could make Saturday evening mass and sleep in on Sunday. I pulled into the cul-de-sac where we lived, the usual street hockey game with parents and kids in process. They parted the ways, I hit the garage door opener and blazed into the garage. In my distracted state I managed to forget about the tree on top of the car. Too late. Drove straight into the garage, sprung the door, then backed out to see how bad, bad was. Really bad. My garage door was hanging from only one of the ten rollers and the garage door opener, dangling over the other car, a Honda Accord.

It's not that I had never used any of those words in anger. But the unique order that emanated from my mouth was, in a word, impressive. Cindy was ushering our grade school-aged boys into the house while trying to explain that "Daddy is just upset." The skating fathers from the street hockey game came over to help. The two of them took one look, and one explained, "We can't do anything with that."

So Cindy took the boys to church and I went on a mission to find an emergency, Saturday evening garage door repair company. Which I found, at $200 per hour plus a fee to drop by at this hour. By the time my family returned from church, the door was already repaired. And about ten years of savings on those Christmas trees had evaporated in one A.D.D. moment.

As luck would have it, we had a party to attend that evening, and of course my wife, now over my little expletive explosion, told the story to a friend. Next thing I heard from the "friend" yelling across the room to me, "Hey, Chevy!" The name stuck. As did "Clark." That's Griswold from *Christmas Vacation* for the three of you who never watched that movie. In the Jahner household it's an annual tradition. Ask my boys their favorite line and out comes "Sh----r was full."

Christmas tree was a little less full that year. Which is what happens when you scrape half of it off with your garage door.

Citibank—St. Louis

Now in St. Louis working with the aforementioned $3 billion mortgage problem, I was Chief of Staff to the Chief Risk Officer of the business. She in time would become the most senior survivor of the mess. Her line bosses, three of them leading up to the company chairman, as well as her dotted-line risk management boss who also reported to the chairman, would all be fired for their incompetence. Our CEO one day walked into her office in the middle of the crisis and commented on how nice it was. We had relocated the department almost a year before that day. So in the midst of the largest mortgage risk crisis the world had ever seen (12 months in at the time and everyone in upper management still in denial), the CEO didn't know where his senior risk officer was working. He should have been camped in her office on a daily basis. I could write a lot about this case study on smart people doing really stupid things. It's a book in and of itself and to this day makes my hair stand on end when I look back. I wrote presentation after presentation to convince the regulators that we were just fine, while at the same time creating presentations for our own senior management trying to convince those knuckleheads that the sky was falling. In today's world, perhaps we could have simply become whistleblowers, turned in the whole lot of them and taken millions home in the form of a commission percentage against what would have been a tremendous fine. Oh well. I didn't really need my own island, anyway.

  I'd prefer to look back on the fun times, which we created in the midst of chaos to retain our own sanity. I turned 40 in that office, and my colleagues happily filled my office with black balloons, about chest high. Cindy was bringing the boys over and I told the two of them I needed their help. Handing each a pin, I told them my office needed to be cleared. It sounded like a machine gun as they happily popped balloons for the next 15 minutes.

  Colleague Bill was a handy target. He was a credit genius who would eventually move on to the restaurant business, having had enough of working with 'difficult' senior management. When he had an ear surgery that temporarily left him deaf, conveniently, on the phone side of his head, we (and by we I mean I) secretly turned down the volume on his phone, then had his secretary call him. I then came around the corner asking, mildly irritated, if he was going to answer his phone. It was at this moment he noticed each of us wearing one giant fake ear in his honor, and realized he had been had. On another occasion, Bill announced that he would never wear a pink shirt, stylish at the time. That's pretty much all we needed. When he went on a business trip we 'pinked' his office. The entire glass front was covered in pink saran wrap. As were the fluorescent lighting covers on the ceiling, casting a nice hue on the whole room. The flock of plastic pink flamingos in the corner was a final touch. What we did not plan was the visit from our three-up boss that happened to occur on the day Bill returned. There was no time to un-pink the place. Nice bit of timing when the boss walked by.

Bibi was another interesting character. Of Lebanese decent, he was once asked if he felt safe in the years he worked in New York City. His reply, "I grew up in Beirut Lebanon. Yes, I feel very safe in New York." His wife was Jordanian, and their two kids had been born in the U.S., so when the family traveled together he would fan out three colors of passports at customs. Always the gentleman, Bibi would look back at people behind him and advise them "You do not want to be in this line."

My friend Jim, who also worked for Citibank in New York, was a stitch. He ran global information for the bank and on one occasion had a memorable exchange with Solomon, a Greek colleague who pronounced Jim's name with that wonderful heavy accent, coming out Jee-mah. The exchange, and imagine the Greek accent:

> Solomon: "You know Jee-mah, I get the feeling that we have gotten off on the wrong foot."
>
> Jim: "I like you Solomon, I just wouldn't trust you as far as I could throw you."
>
> Solomon: "Now Jee-mah, that's just the foot I was talking about."

When traveling together in Florida in the early 90's on a training course, Jim and I were walking at South Beach when it started raining. We ducked into an outdoor/indoor bar/restaurant and ordered, at his request, "something with fruit on it." It would have been handy to be a migrant seasonal farm worker with a spare machete to get through those drinks. Jim would later visit the restroom, and upon return exclaim, "the guy in the men's room putting on makeup was real pretty." Just then Ru Paul arrived. I said, "Do you realize that we just ordered fru-fru drinks in a transvestite bar?" Fun times.

When I was later fired by a Jewish boss on Christmas Eve (no, I'm not making that up), Jim and long-time friend and training associate Art came to the rescue with a job that would eventually take me to Asia for ten years. More on that later. The firing was better received than expected by Cindy, whose first response to the news was "It's about time. He's a jerk." At the time she was right. One of his claims to fame was adorning the filing cabinet in his office with the magnetic name tags of the people he had removed from the company. I was asked to provide three of those name tags when called to reduce staff, and refused. Not well received.

As luck would have it, our paths crossed at a training course in Switzerland a few years later—a course he was taking, and I was teaching, in the job Jim and Art had gotten me after he'd fired me (really). At which time he announced that he now carried the picture of his personality coach in his wallet. The company had sent him to charm school, he told me, and he'd had a baby boy (enter more perspective). We had a nice conversation that I never would have imagined possible back in his nametags-of-the-fallen-on-the-filing-cabinet days.

One final story on Jim, which provided the title for this book: While living in a rent-controlled apartment in New York City, with the absentee owner living in another state, he received a call from his landlord, asking him to send a pinata for a birthday party. Jim, coveting his access to rent far lower than New York City market value, took advantage of the amenities of the city by locating, purchasing and shipping a pinata inside of a lunch break. But, as he would later explain to me, "I bought the ugliest pinata I could find, because *you never want to do anything just right.*" This stuck, becoming something of a family mantra over the years—you might be surprised how well it often it fits a situation. In our family, at least.

Like buying my wife a vacuum cleaner for Valentine's Day. (In my partial defense we needed one and it was a RED vacuum cleaner to match the holiday). I do take full responsibility for the running shoes and exercise bike that were chosen as gifts for her birthday and then Mother's Day that same year. It was a long (well, more than one) year after that.

Or wife Cindy's caring response to the news that I was having my appendix removed in Council Bluffs, Iowa, while we were on a family road trip: "How could you do this to me?" My response: "Wait a minute, a guy named Deek is going to cut into me with a hunting knife and I hurt enough that I don't care, and this is your problem?" In *her* partial defense she did have a one-year-old (sick as well) and three year-old in tow and would be driving them back to St. Louis solo. Besides, I was used to a certain level of sympathy, evidenced before we were married on the day of my second knee injury when she, as I was writhing on the softball field, exclaimed: "Now both knees will match."

Or telling Corey that he would be fine, before then being talked into a trip to the emergency room where his broken collar bone was diagnosed.

Or the loving parents who took their grown sons to a great restaurant in Hong Kong, where the three men of the family contracted food poisoning. The boys are throwing their mother under the bus on this one, as she alone passed on sharing in that last order of scallops.

As you can see from these few examples and, really, every other page in this book, we're fairly expert at never doing anything just right.

Chapter Five

→ Life at the Beach

In 1986, when first son Kyle was two years old and second son Corey was approaching his first birthday, we were introduced to Sunset Beach, a wonderful family island vacation spot at the southernmost tip of North Carolina. Cindy's sister and brother-in-law, Lesley and Joe, had found it through friends Laurie and Rex, whom they'd met while on a corporate stop in, of all places, Milwaukee. They and a number of other couples had met at a newcomer gathering—a get-together for recent residents—and became fast friends. This Milwaukee crew of various professionals, along with family and friends from elsewhere, would begin a two-week pilgrimage to the beach at the same time each year. The group grew over time to incorporate other families and births and extensions, to the point where we peaked with over 100 people from 14 different states. They became our own extended family, watching our kids grow up, one year at a time, together, on one of the best family beaches on the planet.

In those days, the island was accessed via one of the few one-lane, floating swing-open pontoon bridges in the country. It opened on the hour, and on command for commercial watercraft. Charming aspect of the island. Except for the days when it malfunctioned, and you found yourself stranded on one side or the other for 2-3 hours while parts were barged in from 50 miles away for the necessary repairs. In January 2011, the old pontoon bridge swung open for the last time (sealing its history as the last of its kind on the Atlantic Coast) to be replaced by today's causeway bridge. There are to this day residents and vacationers who lament the modernization. Cindy and I are over it, and now enjoy the daily drive over the bridge, high enough to see the ocean to the south over the house tops. Still gives me a lift to see that. This landlocked boy from North Dakota was hooked the first time he saw an ocean.

For many years we made our annual pilgrimage to Sunset Beach from our home in St. Louis in a Honda Accord, with the four of us and a trunk crammed with clothes, beach chairs, toys and the like. I can pack a trunk, and after the tetras exercise was complete, I would challenge anyone to fit a bag of marshmallows in there. These were the days before kids had access to (and needed) videos to get them into a car to travel from home to, say, school, just five minutes away. Kyle and Corey were told, "Bring your books, games, (and eventually) a personal CD player and buck up." Eleven hours from St. Louis to Ashville, North Carolina on day one, six-plus hours on day two to finish the journey. My neighbors in St. Louis would ask, "How do you get your kids to do that? Mine never would." My answer was, "I tell them, 'Get in the car.'"

The boys (and we) loved the beach vacations. After a number of years we asked them if they, like so many of their friends, would like to go to Disney World. At the time we had purchased annual family passes to Six Flags, under a half hour from our house and affording multiple trips to a wonderful amusement park with far shorter lines than a huge international attraction. The boys asked if we would still go to the beach, and we replied no, Disney would have to replace the beach. They talked with each other about it for less than a minute and chose the beach.

Corey would spend his first 20 birthdays at Sunset Beach, and my brother Al and I would take him and older brother Kyle to Las Vegas for his 21st. They acclimated nicely. When Al and I were leaving the lobby of our hotel for a morning tee time, they were just getting in. I never knew any more about their evening, the details of which stayed in Vegas.

Today we reside here in Sunset Beach, North Carolina, having recently moved off the island but staying very nearby. Traded a five-minute walk to the beach for a five-minute drive. The original instigators, Rex and Laurie live on the island. Family Joe and Lesley also live just off the island and another couple, Brian and Caroline from that original group are home owners on the island.

And in even more of a small world story, while living in Singapore we met not one but two couples who own homes on Sunset Beach. This is a small island, with around 100 full time residents. So that six degrees of separation thing was validated with our little sample.

Beach, Bocce and Binging

The group grew to be quite large, so there was always someone to chat with, body surf beside, or kid(s) to play with. Ocean water temperature like a bath. Gradual depth in the ocean and many tidal pools making a perfect alternative for the little ones. At low tide an expansive beach over 100 yards wide with hard-packed sand and minimal shells, which made for epic games of...

Bocce. An Italian lawn bowling game played on a dirt—or in our case, sand—court. Early on, one of our regulars found a bocce game with hard rubber, liquid-filled balls and brought them to the beach. Roll them long or short, lob them into the dunes (pre-ecological interference), play the bounce shot over tide pools and create your own language around the competition. Yellow and green on one team, red and blue on the other. Three simple rules evolved:

1. You must have a counterweight. That would be a beer in your non-throwing hand.

2. Never measure. If you cannot eyeball the point then it's no-mas. Play on.

3. Anyone, at any time, whether or not his team is in control of the point, can call for a re-beer. At which time the game must immediately turn and play toward the coolers.

3b. As we aged, rule 3b was added, allowing for the call of a de-beer, necessitating one or more trips to the AU (Atlantic Urinal). On occasion special consideration would be given for a simultaneous re-de-beer. We weren't heathens, for goodness' sake.

Beach days were planned around the family (they were always at the beach playing every game you can think of, and dad's knees could handle hot box, wiffleball, frisbee, kite flying, on and on), golf (generally in the mornings) and low tide (prime bocce court). Late afternoon low tides were especially welcome, and occasionally dangerous for reasons to follow. All of this would inevitably lead to the occasional....

Binging. One of our regulars was a Miller distributor. So the truck would show up at the beginning of the week with supplies. One year the load peaked at 40 cases of Lite. Which lasted about 10 days. There were a lot of us, eventually all had lost a job here and there thanks to 'right sizing'. And we were thirsty. Really thirsty. And a general beach rule became, if a beer is brought to the beach it is not carried off of the beach. A severe breach of protocol punishable for, let me think, ever. Coolers came full and returned empty. Which ultimately (at times) led to....

Bitching. Yes, our rules occasionally left one or more of us in trouble. But rules are rules. One fine evening as the sun was setting on a low tide/prime bocce court. A brilliant colleague had refilled a large cooler and we did have the rule. So the games continued, eight of us at dusk (i.e. harder to see the object palinka) in serious need of a spotter. Enter five-year old son Kyle who was at an early age particularly adept at calling who was closest to the target. Arm the lad with a flashlight and you have a game. Wife not particularly happy when we returned after nine that night, but Kyle and I were having a great time.

Over time a variety of attire would spring up, primarily around the two separate golf tournaments originated by our group (see Burglar and Memorial section, upcoming). Bocce-related attire was a natural from overseas while I lived there. Caps cost next to nothing in Seoul. So, one year all of my brethren bocce fanatics would receive a 'Sunset Beach Boccie Club' hat, adorned with game attributes, 'Nice Out' stitched on one side (insert your own joke here), and in Korean lettering on the other side, 'God's Game'. No one ever believed that interpretation, but I'm sticking with the story.

He Said What?

Really not certain about including this story. My guess is that Cindy or my editor will veto it. But it will at least make the first draft.

July 16, 1999, John F. Kennedy Jr., son of U.S. President John F. Kennedy, died when the light aircraft he was flying crashed into the Atlantic Ocean off Martha's Vineyard, Massachusetts. Tragic to say the least.

So why mention it here? Well, we happened to be on our annual vacation to Sunset Beach at the time, and all four of us were at the house as the story unfolded. They had already retrieved the body from the underwater wreckage when it was decided, in deference to John's love of the ocean, he should be buried at sea. Without missing a beat, our youngest, 12-year old Corey, asked, "Isn't that like a catch-and-release program?"

Later, at the beach, I relayed the story to the guys on the bocce court, telling them, "I'm proud and afraid at the same time."

He's an attorney today. Go figure.

Burglars and Memorials

Over time, our annual vacations to Sunset Beach saw a significant growth in numbers, which afforded the opportunity to create our own golf tourneys.

The first tournament was not so much planned, but happened as the result of a particular circumstance. In 1994, we had our usual group of suspects on the course when brother-in-law Joe received a call relaying the lousy news that his home in Raleigh had been burglarized. He quickly left the course and returned home to assess the damage. Thankfully the thieves were a couple of fries short of a full order. Nothing of significant value had been taken, save for some electronics that were either easily replaceable, or out of date and on the hit-list anyway. The culprits had fed the dog to keep him quiet, stuck around long enough to enjoy a drink and left without a piece of jewelry or anything of sentimental value. All-in-all not nearly as bad as it could have been. Joe was back at the beach a couple of days later.

The following year, one of our brethren brought can cozies for all in a golf motif, with a caricature of one player teeing off while the rest of the foursome stood by holding various electronics. Titled the 1995 Sunset Beach Burglar Open, the name would stick and become an annual event. Entry fees were collected, and the winning scramble team won all of the money. And paid for all of the post round beers. I made a birdie putt on 18 one year to win it for my team and lost $40. The winnings never covered the bar tab. Best position to finish was second for bragging rights while protecting assets.

A few years later a second tourney was created, the Memorial. Not what you're thinking. This event would memorialize some of our most colorful characters. The theme was to choose a 'mark' who would be the subject of the year's ridicule. Anything from the past vacations that might have been wished by the 'mark' to be forgotten was forever remembered via t-shirts and paraphernalia. A formal presentation occurred at breakfast before the round. Then the current year's mark would choose anonymously the target for the following year. Which would set into motion a year-long quest to get the materials just right.

Chapter Six

→ Life Adventures in Singapore

Working life at Citi to this point had been an adventure, to say the least. Good times and very smart associates (don't look for your names here), business that was successful at times and at others offset by portfolio blowup, for the most part great bosses (a bunch of them, twelve in my first six years—think it was me?), and career doors opening and closing. After my Christmas Eve firing, the job Art and Jim created had me working on simulation-based training (a passion to this day in my consulting business) with risk management courses held every six weeks or so in either Key Biscayne, Florida, or throughout Europe. Nice work if you can get it. I reported to Art in New York, his boss was in Chicago and I was in St. Louis. Just a few frequent flyer miles. Art was a fantastic boss for those two years. I think the only disagreement we ever had was whether the chocolate chip cookies served on breaks at our courses should be crispy or chewy. I preferred chewy, Art crispy. We served crispy.

The job was about to open another big door. To another big adventure.

Sometime after I began doing this training, Art asked me to help out on another training course—in Sydney, Australia. During this trip, I met the South Asia Pacific Chief Risk Officer for Citibank. On a connecting flight back to Singapore, he asked me to move there to oversee risk management training efforts throughout ten countries, from Seoul to Sydney. This was a decision I did not see coming.

Nor did I have an easy time making it.

We had visited Singapore about a year prior on another job assignment. Cindy accompanied me and we stayed with friends from St. Louis who had made the move. So we had some insight into life there.

I pondered all the way home.

The Move

My darling wife, the adventurer, said yes to the idea in about six minutes. The boys were entering sixth and seventh grades and when they discovered that there was baseball and American football available there, along with a highly regarded school, were on board with the idea in about six days. Took me six weeks to make the decision. It would most likely be a two-to-three-year expat assignment, and what then? And how would this play out for my family? Then, the epiphany: I would rather try this and fail than look back with regrets at not having tried at all.

Singapore turned out to be the best thing we ever did as a family. Not that the idea was universally understood by all. My family with North Dakota roots was just a bit taken back, as was Cindy's from Ohio. Reaction among our friends in St. Louis was an interesting mix. At one end of the spectrum were people who had lived overseas, whose first comment was "What a great thing you can do for your kids." They got it. Unlike the other end of the thought process, when a (former) friend actually asked me: "Why would you want to live with a bunch of Chinks?" My filtered response revolved around the adventure, exposure for the boys, educational opportunities, etc. My unfiltered mind was at the same time quietly responding, "To get away from small-minded jerks like you."

So we were off. Like many job changes I had to precede the family to get started. The flight over in August of 1997 necessitated my leaving the annual Sunset Beach vacation a week early. I'll never forget walking across the bridge on the way to the airport and looking back at our group enjoying their beach time. "What in the world are you doing Rod?"

I moved over, came back to bring the boys and started them in school, and left Cindy to sell a house, two cars, pack part of our belongings for storage and prepare the rest for shipment to our new home. She would later lament that her furniture had been on a cruise, but she had never enjoyed one herself.

And so it began. In due course, the two-to-three year thing turned into a full ten, the boys graduated from the Singapore American School before attending undergraduate schools in the states and all of us developed lifelong friendships with some of the most interesting people we could have imagined. I traveled from country to country with a frequency that occasionally had me realize, beyond the fascination of multiple cultures, that my room key wouldn't open the room number from last week's hotel.

There are tipping points in all of our lives and Asia would be mine.

Oops, Lost One

Settled into the serviced apartment, check. Boys enrolled in the American School, check. School bus schedule figured out, check. Wife Cindy just arrived from the states, check. Boys off to school, check. One boy returns, the other not? Oops.

Kyle (seventh grade) had an after-school activity and missed his bus, an easy mistake to make as there were a lot of them. Corey made it back. No one had mobile phones yet, so we got a call from a pay phone at the school from Kyle. He's alone now and needs a bit of help. Cindy decides that, having once made the 30-minute trip to the school from the downtown area via three different freeways, she knows the way. She sets off. She does not know the way, evident when she ends up at the drive-through checkpoint on the way to Malaysia. She was close, missing a single turn. She is in tears (a rare occurrence for her) and trying to find her way to the American School from English-is-a-second language inhabitants of the area. I'm now home from the office, worried about both of them, and trying to remain calm with Corey. I tell him that all will be ok, that I am jumping into a cab to go to the school. Upon arrival there is no Kyle, no Cindy, just a dark school entrance. The cab driver is confused when I ask him to use his mobile phone, a precious item to anyone in this town I would learn, and finally relents. I call the service apartment and Corey is fine, no word from the other two. By the time I get back they have arrived. Cindy somehow figured it all out and our first adventure was complete.

When we told new friends living in Singapore about the situation, more than one said, "Oh that happens all the time to new expats. It's a small island and they eventually turn up."

Can't say that we were quite as relaxed about it at the time, but we were eventually able to laugh about it.

Sir I Have Mango

We didn't need a maid. Most all of the people we met had one, but we didn't. For about six months. Which was the timing that everyone said was the breaking point. The expat apartments and housing that companies paid for (horrifically expensive) were very large, though the kitchens by comparison were postage-stamp sized. And the only room that was not air conditioned, because maids in the estimation of builders did not need air conditioning in a tropical rain forest. Tied in with this general theme, refrigerators were generally small, and shopping for meals was a daily event, requiring one-to-multiple stops at different locations for the various needs. Grocery store for staples, wet market for meat or fish, often yet another location for fresh fruit and veggies. Service people for the expat homes came relatively often so someone needed to be there to receive them. So day-to-day chores were much more time-consuming and, as maids from abroad were relatively cheap, it made perfect sense to have one. And having one freed up spouses to run their own businesses or, in the case of Cindy, to allow ample time for all of her volunteer work.

Cindy found Nellie on the advertising board at The American Club, and we would employ her for over nine years. This made for a great lifestyle. Like all of the maids, she lived on site with us, though never that visible as the maid's quarters were in the back of the homes, and some of the accommodations were in a word, appalling. An outside, tile room sometimes not even large enough for a single bed. The maid's bathroom was oftentimes the size of a closet, in some cases would have a shower head placed in the middle of the room or over the commode. Ridiculous really. Some of the locals were particularly non-caring (kindly said) for the benefits of their 'servants.' They generally paid half of what the expats did, and treated them as little more than slaves. When we looked at homes we always took interest in the maid's quarters, something that local realtors did not understand.

The first day we had Nellie, I returned from work to find my clothes all perfectly laundered, with even the undershirts and work-out gear ironed. I personally thought my workouts were much more effective in crisply ironed gear. Believe it or not, since repatriation Cindy has not duplicated that protocol. However, for the first two weeks back at the beach, we were notably the only family with ironed t-shirts.

Cindy taught Nellie what we liked to eat, some new tips on food preparation and very soon we had wonderful meals with fresh ingredients every day. We still miss the dried-chili chicken. Nellie was advised that she was not in our home to raise the boys. That was our job and while she did not need to worry about that aspect of the family life, she grew to care for them deeply. Like most expat maids (and unlike most local maids) she had Saturday night through

Sunday off. Most of the help was from either Indonesia, or as in Nellie's case, the Philippines. She sent all of her spare money home, where it largely funded two siblings' schooling. Mornings always began with fresh fruit for me, and Nellie would have a baggie with four or five selections pre-cut to take to the office. Periodically, when she found the perfect Philippine variety of my favorite fruit, she would announce "Sir, I have mango." Which you couldn't just stuff into a baggie with the other fruit. No, the mango would be perfectly cut in moon shaped slivers and arranged in a star pattern on a plate for me. For that I would take time to sit. God, I loved that woman. Cindy, like pretty much every other expat woman, wanted our maid to repatriate with us to the US. A few actually did. Ours didn't (the boys were well into college by now and much of the need for that luxury had passed) but thankfully Nellie moved on to an even better situation where she supervised other maids. That said, as my older brother would predict, not having her around created something of a hard landing back in the states. We all remember her fondly.

Sir YOU Have....

Friend John and his family lived in a house near an undeveloped wooded area (ok, jungle). In his backyard was a staircase with a large concrete drain running alongside. The drain was protected by small slabs of concrete about 12x18 inches and a couple of inches thick. One morning he came outside to find that someone had lifted one of the slabs off at the top of the staircase. And his cat had become stuck inside the drain. With a bit of tugging, he was able to free his pet. When he noticed that the hair on the front half of the cat's body was slicked back, his maid said, "Sir, you have snake." Whereupon John did what any dedicated expat would do. He asked his wife to call the snake patrol and left for the office. As it turns out he had pulled his cat out of the mouth of a very large python which had crawled up the drainage area, popped the concrete slab off and snatched his meal. The snake patrol, (it took about six of them to wrangle what turned out to be a seven or eight foot monster with a body the size of a man's thigh) asked his wife if she would like to participate in a picture.

She said no.

To Cane or Not to Cane

Without a doubt the most asked question when we would tell someone new that we moved to Singapore is "Isn't that the place where they cane people?" Of course they were referring to a fairly famous situation where a student of the American School received the punishment for stealing signs and (apparently disputed) spray painting cars in parking lots. Six strokes of the cane was the punishment, reduced to four after intervention by President Clinton. It is brutal? You bet. It is not public. But this is no garden variety spanking. Most pass out from the pain after six strokes. My first thought was if not for the vandalism, then the stupidity of a teen certainly rated being a contributing factor. If you live in Singapore for more than about 20 minutes and don't realize that you are being videoed pretty much everywhere, you're clueless. Vandalism, and many crimes of destruction are rare compared to other large cities, and for good reason. We had someone scratch the walls of one of our office elevators one day and with help of the pin hole camera in the ceiling the perpetrator was caught in twenty-four hours. This was in the 90's. Today caning is generally reserved for more serious offences, such as rape or assault.

Punishment for serious crimes is swift and severe. The embarkation card you fill out to enter the country advises DEATH TO DRUG TRAFFICKERS. They are not kidding. In one instance a mule who had consumed heroin balloons was flying through Changi Airport, passed them in the airport and was waiting for his accomplice. Who was late so the mule hung around the airport for 24 hours, drew attention to himself and was arrested. The mule gave up the accomplice, and both were given death sentences by hanging within two weeks. Guess what, there wasn't too much of a drug problem there.

We had an expat kid in our football program who was rumored to be getting involved with drugs. Commissioning at the time, I advised his dad that if true, he needed to get the situation under control. The dad found it hard to believe that anyone who is caught with drugs in an amount deemed more than sufficient for personal consumption, they are considered a dealer. As an accommodation to expat families, if one of their kids was caught with drugs, the entire family would be given the opportunity to leave the country within 24 hours and send back for their belongings. And this is an invitation that should be accepted. They really don't mess around.

There was an exception to the severity rule. On one occasion a 'gentleman' murdered his wife and before accompanying his mistress to a wedding in Malaysia, left the door to the apartment ajar, radio blaring so someone would discover the body with his alibi securely in place across the border. Upon return after the weekend, the door was still ajar, radio still blaring, wife still dead. Whereupon he made up a story that was seen through by the police in about five minutes. He then called the whole thing a crime of passion as his wife had called his mother a tramp and sister a whore. He received seven years in prison. So a few of us got to thinking, "you know.....with seven years to do nothing but look after your portfolio and no expenses...."

Stop it. I was joking. Really.

Golf in Malaysia

We chose to join a country club in Malaysia given the prohibitive expense of doing so in Singapore. Palm Resort was beautiful, with three eighteen-hole courses, two restaurants, full locker room facilities, steam room, hotel and pools. About a thousand dollars a year covered our family of four with $18 cart fees for each round. We spent a lot of time there.

The drive over was not bad, 45 minutes door to door, with drive-through customs check points at each country's border. There they verified passports, took your pre-completed embarkation form, occasionally searched the trunk, drew a little money out of a cash card and sent you on your way. The roadway on the Malaysia side was new and pristine, with three toll booths that also were quick drive-throughs when you made sure you had the coins in local currency available to pitch into the bin. And on occasion one or two of Malaysia's finest would set up cones on the roadway to collect an alternate toll, generally from those of us who had an 'S' as the beginning letter on our license plates, meaning we were from Singapore. We all had entertaining stories about this little business proposition.

Our first such encounter was when we were being visited by Aunt Lesley and our niece Ali. Cindy, Lesley and Ali rode and I drove. All was going normally until I saw the cones I had heard about just ahead. I stopped and one of the two policemen proceeded to write my license number down on a very official looking napkin. At my request Cindy had pulled out a single bill from the local currency envelope and place the rest back in the glove compartment. Sadly, in this case the smallest bill was 100 Ringgit, or about $25. I had been advised that 50 Ringgit was the going rate. The exchange that followed was brief and to the point:

> Policeman: "You were going veddy fast."
>
> Me: "How fast?"
>
> Policeman: "125 over (kilometers per hour, speed limit was 110. The number was nowhere close but apparently 125 was the speed of the day)
>
> Me: "No receipt boss."
>
> Policeman: "No receipt."
>
> I handed him the 100 Ringgit note and we were on our way. Upon departure this conversation followed:
>
> Ali: "Oh my God, Uncle Rod just bribed a police officer. Were you scared?"
>
> Me: "Not really. I've been told how this works. Actually, I was irritated because we didn't have a 50 and they don't make change."
>
> Ali: "I was going to take a picture but didn't have time."

Me: "Oh no, no, that wouldn't have been a good idea. Uncle Rod might have been gone for a long time."

My friend Bob had an entertaining version of this little dance. When pulled over he elected to push back. Their exchange:

>Policeman: "You were going veddy fast."
>
>Bob: "How fast?"
>
>Policeman: "One twenty-five over."
>
>Bob: "That's not how fast I was going."
>
>Policeman: "We have picture."
>
>Bob: "Show me."
>
>Policeman produces a picture, with speed on the bottom.
>
>Bob: "That's not the number."
>
>Policeman: "Picture just like this."
>
>Bob: "That's not my car."
>
>Policeman: "Picture just like this."
>
>Bob: "It's not even the color of my car."
>
>Policeman: "Picture just like this."
>
>Bob: "Can't you just show me something close?" Fine paid, Bob was on his way. He had the foresight to have a 50 on hand.

Another on my front. One day I was driving over alone to play golf, and the checkpoint on the Malaysia side was grossly undermanned. This happened occasionally when one or the other country was mad about something. So the usual 5 minute wait turned into 45, which made me dangerously close to missing my tee time. Once on the highway in Malaysia, I stepped on it. And as luck would have it, this was also a day for an alternative toll setup. I saw the lone policeman this time in the distance beginning to set up his cones, not yet blocking traffic. So, I decided not today, and stepped on it a little harder. When I passed him, I was at about 150 kph and climbing. Even at that speed the size of his eyeballs were clearly growing. His pants ruffling in my rearview mirror, I continued on without incident and made my tee time. Had a 50 Ringgit note along that time, too. Pity.

Mumbai Prescription

On one of my early trips to India, I contracted India belly. It was the second such event out of five trips there to that point in time. I had been so careful, never setting foot out of the five-star hotel (the meeting was onsite and they often have their own additional filtration systems for the notoriously poor water), ate nothing that wasn't peeled by me, no salads nor anything else that could have been washed in the water, kept my mouth tightly closed in the shower, used hand sanitizer, the whole drill. In retrospect I believe it was one of the sauces at a dinner which may have been uncooked before serving. Whatever the case I was in need of drugs to kill the little invaders within.

I noted that there was a 'Chemist' on the premises. Their name for a pharmacy. It was closed at the time so I went to the front desk, where the head bellman was standing. I asked if the Chemist was going to be open today, to which he replied that he should be already, so he would 'be right in.' Which in local parlance means sometime between the next hour and a week from Tuesday. I then asked if antibiotics were sold in India without a prescription (a practice in more than one Asian country). He said yes, immediately pulled out a pad of paper, and the hotel bellman was now going to write my prescription. This exchange followed:

> Bellman: "What would you like?"
>
> Me: "Amoxicillin."
>
> Bellman: "Two-fifty or five-hundred milligram?"
>
> Me: "Five-hundred."
>
> Bellman: "Eight tablets enough?"
>
> Me: "Yes. Can you deliver to my room?"
>
> Bellman: "Yes."

Fifteen minutes later one of his runners was at my room, medication in hand (in the same familiar packaging as seen in the states) and charging me the equivalent of three U.S. dollars. Including tip.

Don't get me started on the cost of health care. After repatriating I travelled back to Malaysia for a consulting assignment, and went to a pharmacy in a shopping mall in Kuala Lumpur. One particular medication that Cindy was taking was costing us $100 per month. I bought the very same dosage, in verified packaging and paid about $50 for a six-month supply.

Diabetic Boy

Corey went Type I or Juvenile Diabetic when a freshman in high school. A scary time, to which I won't subject you to the details. While in the hospital a "nutritionist" was saying things like "for breakfast he can have a half of a bagel." She was shown the door. This was a growing athlete who was wondering if he would be able to play sports again. Enter Coach Mike, who was in the midst of tryouts for the travel baseball team. I called him, advising that we didn't know what we were dealing with as regards competitive sports in the near term and that he would miss the tryouts. Without hesitation, Mike replied, "You tell Corey that he doesn't need tryouts, and he better get well quick because we need him in Perth." That put a sparkle back in his eyes. From the start he managed his disease, never once needing us to administer insulin shots, which over time have ranged from three to four per day. We went to Perth, and he had a great tourney while periodically asking me for food to be delivered to the dugout as he was learning the feeling of going low in blood sugar upon exertion. And in another small world story, much later in life Coach Mike would become part of our extended family as his son Sean, Corey's teammate, married one of my nieces after meeting her at Corey's older brother's wedding. Can't make this stuff up.

The term Diabetic Boy, not his mother's favorite, was given to him by a friend who in return was affectionately referred to as (Another kind of, censored for self-preservation purposes) Boy. Boys will be boys.

We walked on eggshells to a degree, trying not to hover while worrying about Corey. He took it all in stride, and at one point we had to remind him that insulin shots were not necessarily a spectator sport. This after a call from the maître d at one of the American Club restaurants called Cindy to relay the "go, go, go" chants of his friends as they rooted on his self-administration of the necessary medication.

Sometime after Corey's disease set in, Cindy contracted cancer and was in need of a major surgery. (Spoiler alert—surgery was successful and she remains cancer-free to this day). At the dinner table one night, Cindy relayed news of the surgery, and that while chances were slim, there is always the possibility of life ending complications. The boys were stunned to silence at that prospect. Until Corey piped up with, "Mom, if you die, we will really miss you. But can I have your pancreas?" After the laughter subsided, we realized that a weight had been lifted, and from that point on we were all a bit more relaxed about "the beedies" as he calls it.

Shout out here to The Juvenile Diabetes Association for the great work being done to understand this disease. When Corey first contracted diabetes, there was speculation that a cure might be in the cards in five or so years. That time frame has become a rolling five-year clock, with much progress along the way to assist in managing the affliction. We continue to pray for a cure.

Cigars

I had smoked the occasional cigar prior to moving overseas, but now Cubans were in the mix. Some of which I found to be quite a treat. There were a number of us who shared the same minor addiction. My neighbor's humidor was a converted China cabinet. When we first met, he offered me a smoke, asking if I preferred "something short, medium or a commitment?" The commitment was a Churchill, the size of which was not unlike, let me think, a sequoia.

We all had stories of bringing cigars home, and passing through customs. The chances of being pulled over for a bag search were relatively remote, but sooner or later your number came up. And not too many of the agents cared if you were bringing a box or two for personal use. I had my carry-on searched in San Francisco one day, and the agent looked right at a box of Romeo and Julieta's, said nothing and zipped the pocket closed.

My brother also enjoyed the occasional good cigar, and our routine for stopping to play in his member guest tournament when returning stateside was for him to pay my entry fee into the tournament and me to bring him a box of his favorite cigars. It got to the point after a couple of years that when I knocked on his door, he would open it a couple of inches, wait for me to show him the Cubans and then allow me entry to his home.

Some of the more colorful such stories came from my friend Bob. While connecting through Minneapolis, he was selected for inspection. The customs agent asked "Sir, is there anything you wish to declare?" Bob responded, "No." The agent then opened all of the many zippers on the carry-on, and spotting a box of Cubans in one of them, again asked "Sir, is there anything you wish to declare?" Bob responded, "Nope." Whereupon the agent quietly closed the zipper and sent him on his way. On a subsequent connection from overseas again through Minneapolis some six weeks later, the odds were defied by being again pulled over for inspection. Further defying the odds, it was the same customs agent, who recognized Bob no doubt for that memorable exchange. So he asked "Sir, is there anything you wish to declare?" Bob responded, "Nope." Whereupon the agent asked him, "Sir, is there any particular zipper you would like me not to open?" Bob pointed to the one containing the box of Cubans and said, "That one right there."

A pilot friend of Bob's would then one-up the story. His acquaintance had purchased for the first time a box of Churchills (see sequoia above), and was selected for inspection in Minneapolis. The particular customs agent was a bit less forgiving, perhaps because he himself was being watched. In any case the agent pulled out the Churchills and announced, a bit sadly, that he would need to destroy them. Now this was about a $400 box of cigars and he knew it. He then took the cigars out, very carefully cut each of them exactly in half, returned them to the box and gave the box back to the traveler, announcing "There, they are destroyed and you can continue on your travels." So in essence, in the act of 'destroying' a box of Churchills, he gave the passenger two boxes of Robustos (cigars roughly the size of half a sequoia).

Smallest World

I challenge anyone to beat this small world story. And not the first time the story has found its way into a book. (A fuller version was published in *Close Encounters of the Fargo Kind* by Marc de Celle, a book that captures the essence of people from North Dakota): After moving to Singapore, a new superintendent of the Singapore American School (SAS) was hired. One Bob Gross from Napoleon, North Dakota, not 15 miles away from Linton,

North Dakota where I was born. Bob had retained that heavy German brogue, so to listen to him appeared a bit out of place geographically. But make no mistake, he would prove to be a magnificent choice for that job. Best school superintendent I ever met. When Bob talked to you, you were the center of his universe. He looked you in the eye and you could see the concentration and pure interest in your words. And even if the next time you saw him was some-time later, he remembered every detail about you, your family, anything that came out of that first encounter. This is one of his many gifts that all who encountered the man noticed. He truly is relationship driven to his core.

It gets better. On my next home-leave I told this story to a cousin, who immediately turned thoughtful on me, as if you could see the wheels turning. He said, "Bob Gross....I think Bob's grandfather was Rafael, and I know that Rafael was your Dad's Mother's First Cousin." Which prompted me to ask him if he knows the entire family tree of the state of North Dakota. (Insert your own joke here; how many twigs can there be on that tree?)

Upon return to Singapore I happened to be at a dinner function where Mr. Gross was in attendance. I wandered over to his table and asked, "Bob, is your grandfather Rafael?" He looked as me a bit puzzled before answering in the affirmative. I replied, "Well, hello, cuz." And in true North Dakota fashion his next words were "I knew you were from good stock."

Football Where You Don't Expect It

One of the pleasant surprises for my boys when we moved to Singapore was the existence of the Singapore American

Football League (SAFL). This was an all-volunteer program, started in the mid 70's by the oil patch expats who wanted something positive for the kids. They went to their respective companies who ponied up funds and put it all together. There were three age-based leagues, the American (fifth and sixth graders), National (seventh, eighth and small ninth graders) and World (high school). There were generally 3-4 teams in each league, each with 2-4 coaches, team moms, announcers for game day, videos of every game for film night, cheerleaders, the works. Add it all up and there were over 100 volunteers who year after year made the program work. An annual exchange game with Korea (where the military bases had teams) was a highlight for the high school teams. Just after my boys graduated, the Japan American School was added. After our time trips to and from Okinawa and Guam, and more recently plans for London and/or Australia.

   I, like many, volunteered to help when the boys played. Spent quite a few Saturdays watching them play from the best seat in the house, working the chain gang. Later I would gravitate to refereeing, in the process learning a new appreciation for how difficult that job can be. We were paid to referee, all the free Gatorade you could drink in the sweltering heat.

   The coaches hated each other for about two hours a week on game day, then gathered at someone's home for post-game partying and reliving of the day's games. It was a great group of guys, giving of themselves for the kids and enjoying each other's company. At one of those parties, someone asked for a beer to be sent down the table to him. As it passed by, I grabbed it for myself, also in need. He exclaimed "Hey, that was a nice interception. You'd make a good commissioner." Got a good laugh but little did I foresee that a year later when the current commissioner repatriated, I was asked to fill the seat. For the first year my friend John helped me with the task, which involved finding league commissioners and coaches and the rest of the volunteers, managing equipment handout and collection, overseeing league drafts, settling disputes, keeping the manual up to date with playing and league rules, etc. It would be a job I would keep for seven years, with the longest tenure before me at three. In my year of departure this would earn me, 1) a nice plaque from the athletic association thanking me for my service and, 2) an exact replica of that plaque from the World League coaches that dubbed me the "Dumbass of the Decade". It reads, "What Kind of Drooling Idiot stays on as SAFL Commissioner for 7 Years? Presented with Great Affection From the World League Coaches." They put a lot of thought into that plaque. These were some of the best men I ever had the privilege to work with, and many remain lifelong friends.

There are a million stories from those days, from poignant to hysterical, touching to sad, fun to angst. And I wouldn't give up a minute of any of it. The best tribute I could think of at the time of my departure is in excerpts from my goodbye speech at my final opening ceremony:

"Someone asked me recently why I would do this job for seven years. I responded that I did not sign up for eight... Actually, this has truly been a labor of love.

My first memory telling me what this league is all about occurred before I was commissioner. While refereeing an American League playoff game, a head coach called time out. His team was behind by six, it was late in the game and the opposition had the ball deep in their own territory. One of his players had just made a great stopping tackle and I expected a 'we need the ball' fire and brimstone meeting from the coach. Instead, he helped his battered player to his feet and said enthusiastically, 'Great hit! Isn't this fun?' I was hooked from that day forward.

When asked to be here today I did a word association with a couple of former players. 'I say SAFL, what do you say?'

One relayed the following: Football. In a place you wouldn't expect it. Oilers (his team). Domination. Our Coach Donalson's Converse shoes. Ref Johnson's short shorts. Coach Matison having a mild conniption. Practice and games in sweltering weather meant only for preseason, not an entire freaking season.

The other was more succinct: I say I miss High School Football.

Those two boys are my sons, each of whom played for six years in the SAFL. My wife Cindy and I can still hear one of them after a particularly tough practice, upon entering the house and whimpering, 'Make the bad man stop'. The bad man didn't stop and believe me they learned more than how to play football. They became better people. When they return to Singapore, one of the first calls they make is to their former coach. And that is what they call him. He always was and always will be, simply, Coach.

Then I asked a number of coaches, referees and commissioners to tell me what the SAFL means to them. A collection of their thoughts include:

- "...impressive volunteer members of the American community that are teaching way more than how to play football....people that make the opportunity for our kids to play the greatest game known to man and kids playing that incredibly demanding game in tough circumstances." This coming from a man who once ran the same running play to the left, 13 times in a row. When asked about it later, he replied 'I was going to run it until they stopped it. And next week we might run to the right.'

- "The SAFL is a unique opportunity....a game that I feel teaches life lessons (teamwork, individual responsibility, decision making and strategy) that can't be duplicated in other games." This man routinely referees two games in the heat before coaching on the sidelines in the same day. He lost so much weight last year that he dropped two hat sizes.

- "...the opportunity to contribute in a meaningful way to the growth and development of the young people in my charge, far beyond blocking and tackling." This coach, even after decades of contributions to our kids, continues giving tirelessly. (And when coaching on game day, he is more than happy to share his superior knowledge of the rules of football with the referees on the field.)

These three examples, who by the way have collectively given over 60 years to our kids, all remain humble. They use phrases like 'proud to be associated', 'my bond to the American community in Singapore', 'experience in this league has enriched my life beyond description' and 'my time has been rewarded many times over'. They get a free Gatorade if they ref a game.

...Pride. Responsibility. Team. I've seen coaches in this league bench star players in the playoffs because they weren't happy with behavior in practice or off the field. Life lessons always come first.

A good friend, also with a long SAFL association, recently asked me to write something to his son, a former player, on the occasion of his 21st birthday. The topic was 'What It Means to Be a Man'... I looked no further than the SAFL and gave him a few examples.

- I reminded him of the selfless volunteers here, coaching and refereeing day after day in the heat, some for 10, 20, even 30 years, all for the love of the game and the life lessons that it imparts.

- I told him about a former player on duty in Iraq, who recalled that his coach had military experience. He was scared and called to ask for advice. The soldier would later tell his coach that the advice given on that day had saved his life. The coach, one of the toughest men I have ever known, cannot tell the story without tears in his eyes.

- I relayed a story about a player from 1985-86 who just last year wrote to me, wanting to reconnect with his coach. He said 'SACAC football...was one of the great experiences of my life. One of the reasons it was so special had to do with the coaching staff. After all these years, I would really like to thank Coach for all his effort, dedication and enthusiasm.'

These are the kinds of people that I have had the honor and privilege to work with, and can also proudly call my friends. They and others like them have made this league great, with a 30+ year proud tradition. It seems to me that we are well positioned for another 30 years.

I have a wish for each side of the stands. Players, when the bad man won't stop, there is a good reason. In the words of the namesake of the Rob McCrae Coaches Award, 'Suck it up.' You will be better for it, and you will be able to walk with your head a little higher. Parents, take this from someone who knows. Those players on the other side of the stands will be grown and gone in a heartbeat. Find a reason to be here. Volunteer, if you haven't done so already, to work with the great people that make this league so special. And if you are on this island on game day, come to the stadium and watch every minute of your son's games. I did, and have no regrets now that my boys are on to the next phase of their lives.

I guess this hasn't been such a long seven years after all. I have said this before and will say it again. The SAFL helped turn my boys into young men. I could never repay that debt. To steal a line from Friday Night Lights, my heart is full."

The boys had turned into very good football players over the years. Kyle started lifting weights in the seventh grade, and continually worked on his game to the point that a coach on another team told his players "if you want to be a football player, practice like number 42 over there." He would become a feared hitter and very good tight end, winning the 'Nobles Award' given to one senior each year for courage, dedication, and sportsmanship. Corey's natural athleticism was on display as a quarterback and linebacker. His senior team, an unusually good set of athletes for that environment would be the second team in 12 years to beat Korea where the program was routinely 2-3 times larger than ours. It was a reasonably good game for Corey with an interception at free safety, touchdown at fullback, returned punts and kickoffs, and was the holder for extra points. Other than that, he didn't have much to do. Actually, really nothing to do for a while when, he broke his collarbone with seven minutes left in a game that was out of reach. It gets weirder, as you'll see in Chapter Eleven.

Baseball Where You Don't Expect It Either

The baseball program in Singapore was also an all-volunteer effort with leagues across multiple age groups. Like the football program there was an annual draft in the three age-based leagues, and a dedicated group of volunteers filling various roles.

Saturdays were spent in the stands watching the games and meeting parents of other ball players, many of whom would become close friends to this day. In that regard, the lifestyle was not unlike being in the states, a welcome touch of home.

For a couple of years I helped out good friend Bob as an assistant coach. There was a liberal sprinkling of talent levels on every team and reasonable parity as a result. After each game we would get together, review the team performance and either (a) have a beer while creating the lineups for the next week, or (b) in the case of not having played a very good game, replace the beer with gin. One year in particular, we drank more gin than beer.

There were so many entertaining stories that came out of our time with baseball. My personal favorite was when I was coaching first base, Bob coaching third, and our fastest player on base at first. I knew Bob would be sending him to steal second base. I told him, Marcus, watch your signs.

Bob signaled the steal sign, and Marcus stayed put. Again I offered, Marcus, watch your signs. Another steal sign. Another hold at first. Then Bob, loud enough for the entire complex to hear yells across the diamond "Marcus, STEAL!" He took second base on the next pitch, standing up with two steps to spare while the opposing coaches were crying with laughter.

On an annual basis a rotating five country tournament was held, with three levels of boy's baseball and one high school girls' softball team. So twenty teams in total descended upon the host city each year. Locations were: Singapore; Jakarta, Indonesia; Manilla, Philippines; Bangkok, Thailand, and Perth, Australia. Instead of piling into the minivan for a tourney, we took our passports. The only location we never visited was the International School in Jakarta, who in our last couple of years were scheduled to host but sadly were forced to cancel due to civil unrest. Well, one year it was actually a military coup, a reasonable excuse I suppose. In those years Perth came to the rescue, so we visited there for three years running. To their credit they changed the venue each year so the experience offered differing looks at the region. When we weren't watching baseball, we either golfed or toured various wineries in the Swan Valley and or favorite anywhere, Margaret River.

Sidebar, when you travel to Australia, they are very strict about what you might bring into their country. Golf clubs and shoes are particular targets, all of them checked for dirt that could carry unwanted microbes. So they will make you wait while they clean off whatever you didn't. One of our coaches exclaimed, "I wonder how much I should tip the airport security guy for cleaning my golf shoes."

One year the tournament schedule was perfect in that games generally started at 10am, which allowed friend Darrell and me to play golf every day beforehand. We were at the clubhouse at dawn, often waiting for the pro who let us out first as a twosome. Rounds were routinely completed in under three hours and were accompanied by kangaroos hopping beside our golf cart as we rode. It was like playing in Jurassic Park.

Sadly the second of the years in Perth was the time that my stepfather Walter passed away. He had been failing and had a wonderful life, married over 25 years to two women, one my mother. Walt and Sally enjoyed 31 years together. When he passed I happened to be in a casino in Perth with another friend, on a reasonably good run at blackjack. The call to my mobile phone came in at 2am (late tournament games that trip). So here I am, as far away from Bismarck, ND as you can be without either being in an ocean, or visiting Antarctica. I left the casino, and by 4am was in a car to the airport for a 6am flight to begin the excursion home. Perth to Sydney to L.A. to Denver to Bismarck. 30 hours door to door. At the same time my brother and sister-in-law were making arrangements to travel home from Santa Fe, New Mexico. They beat me by six hours. I told them they needed a better travel agent.

The following year in Perth was special. Our high school team was comprised of all juniors and below. In a cruel twist of fate Kyle had been aged out of the tourney by an archaic rule that was not ruled in his favor because, at least in part, they thought he was too big and strong. Corey played and expectations were not too high. But they peaked at the right time, played great and ended up winning the tournament. Dubbed the 'Regulators', the celebration was epic and involved the players taking turns shaving Coach's head. There was also a shaving incident that involved Kyle's considerable chest/stomach hair that will be reserved for private conversation. Corey had a superb tourney, culminating with back to back homers in the championship game. Which I have on video. Great fun.

9/11

An awful time in our history. One of those that we all remember where we were, our personal and family circumstances, glued to the TV in disbelief and horror.

I happened to be in a Muslim country, Indonesia, working on a training course for the local bank middle managers. The attacks unfolded at 8pm there, being 11 hours ahead. Cindy called me on my mobile as I entered my hotel room after the day's work and told me to turn on the TV. I sat at the edge of the bed and watched while we stayed on the phone.

People would later ask me about whether I felt safe, what the attitude of the people was, all of the questions you might expect. Acquaintances from home who had not travelled as much as we had seemed particularly concerned. My response was two-fold. First, when I announced in the training room the next morning that for the obvious reasons I would only be in training for my segments and would spend the rest of the time in my room gathering updates. The look on the faces of my colleagues stays with me to this day. They didn't know what to say, and felt awful for me and my country.

Back in Singapore on the first school day after the towers came down, local press parked outside of the

American School to ask entering students about their thoughts on the matter. Who should they choose but Kyle? Fortunately, the superintendent would quickly put a stop to the television presence.

Sometime later I would be asked by a family member by way of a forwarded post (so it must be reliable) if a good Muslim can be a good American. The post gave ten reasons that the answer is no, with sweeping generalities in the form of one-liners that spanned theology, geography, philosophy and to some extent, just plain hatred. My response:

"Just another over-simplification of a much more complex issue. And I am certain written by someone who hasn't ventured beyond the end of his driveway to understand people in this world. I had many Muslim friends in Asia. I was in Jakarta on 9/11. And I doubt that they were out to conquer me or anyone else. They were, and are, just like the rest of us. People working for a living, trying to make a better life for their children, and oftentimes disturbed when atrocities occur, just like us. The look of pity on the faces of my friends in Jakarta on that day were genuine.

The problem with this dribble is that these days anyone can write anything, using any sweeping generality that they either come up with on their own, or by adjusting something that has already been written to fit their twisted logic. Then watch happily as others spread their words without verification.

Final note on the topic, fast forwarding to another small world story. An engineer I would meet and play a little golf with in Singapore would go on to rebuild the train station at Ground Zero. After the fountains, museums and new structures were completed we toured it all with our wives.

If you have not done so it should be on your bucket list. He is one of the toughest and brightest people I know, and upon exiting the museum he would remark, "I'm glad we went, but never again. It was too hard."

Sunday Morning Panic

The mind does funny things sometimes. Not long after 9/11, we were living in a house one block away from the American School. It was a large home, with bedrooms on the second and third floors. And made of concrete.

Singapore is a good friend of the U.S., and had quickly sanctioned the posting of machine gun toting Nepalese Gurkhas at the entrances of the American Embassy, American Club and the American School. By now everyone had become comfortable with them as fixtures. When we entered the school I told the boys to "wave to the nice man with the machine gun."

Then I awoke one Sunday morning to the sound of gunfire. Which given recent history and the presence of high-rise housing complexes across the street from both our home and the school was a bit disconcerting. In point of fact the Singaporean government routinely had visited and verified the occupants of the housing complex that otherwise could provide a vantage point. But again, I heard gunfire. Very nearby. Which I'm familiar with as I grew up a hunter.

I awoke Cindy and told her what I had heard. She immediately told me to go to the boy's rooms and make sure they stayed away from the windows. Which was useless because (1) they were teenage boys who could sleep through a tornado, and (2) their beds were in very large bedrooms and already as far away from the windows as they could be anyway.

Something was not right. (Insert understatement of your own here). Another retort, sounding like it was right outside of our bedroom window. But not the sound of a rifle. More like a shotgun. So I edged over to the window and peaked out. Down on the street was, and I am not making this up, the crow patrol. They hated the large black crows that tried to survive there. The chosen method of eradication was a team of two in a truck about the size of our dining room table, armed with a shotgun and fishing rod. They would shoot the birds out of the trees, the latest one not 20 feet from our bedroom window. It had fallen into the large, fenced-in storm drain that ran along the house. So they used the fishing rod to hook it, reel it in, throw it into the truck and continue the hunt.

Ambulance Ride

I threw my back out one fine evening, dropping to the marble floor in our living room like a bad habit. Unable to move and hoping to work my way through the episode, I iced it (well, Cindy iced it) and spent the rest of the night in that position. No relief in the morning and still unable to get up, Cindy called an ambulance. That morning Kyle was on his way to a school interim trip, bicycling in Spain as memory serves, and said goodbye as he bent down to meet me eye to eye on the floor.

The ambulance service was a private one, not uncommon in Singapore. Two guys who had a combined weight of a fourth grader brought in a gurney and told me to get on it. My face still pasted to the marble, I said "the reason I'm down here and we called you is that I cannot move. What's your next plan?"

Plan B was to pick me up with a tarp, which they laid beside me and I very gingerly slid onto. Now it's time to pick me up and place me on the gurney, which was accomplished by the two men, Cindy and our maid Nellie each picking up a corner of the tarp. The ride to the hospital was about 25 minutes, not a pleasant one. Cindy followed in our car.

Once in the emergency room and waiting for a doctor, the ambulance driver is standing over me asking for payment. Dumfounded, I asked how much he needed. S$60, around U.S. forty bucks. Trying to undo my pretzel imitation I painfully reached into my pocket (Cindy had not arrived yet) and gave him his money.

The cost of the ambulance was not much higher than a cab ride of the same distance. So I asked the driver, "the next time it's raining and I can't get a cab, can I call you guys?" No response, no reaction. Another piece of my best material gone to waste.

Leaving and Welcome Home

Ten years almost to the day, it was time to repatriate. Weather for those ten years was like a St. Louis summer every day, 365 days per year. If you want to be a great meteorologist, move to Singapore. The only forecast ever: 28-32 degrees Celsius (82-90 degrees Fahrenheit), around a thousand percent humidity with a chance of thunderstorms. Call it in and go on vacation.

My definition of acclimatization: You still sweat just as much; you just don't care. After growing up in North Dakota, it took all ten of those years to thaw out. Today I figure my lifetime average body temperature is just about right.

Our belongings were crammed into a 40-foot-tall container for the boat ride home. Cindy said her furniture was again afforded a cruise, why not her? Upon arrival in the states, our container was chosen for search. From top to bottom, side to side. Whereupon I received a call from Customs advising me that there was an unacceptable piece of wood on a decoration that must be destroyed. After a bit of back-and-forth, I realized what they had found in that container. It was a Christmas decoration—a painted tree with a round wood tree-limb base about 3 inches across. Buried in a box of other decorations. One box among hundreds. Stuffed behind stacks of furniture. In a container that had room for maybe, just maybe, a t-shirt. This dangerous piece of wood had been a gift in the states from sister-in-law Lesley around 20 years prior. The wood had long been petrified, traveled across the pond twice and whatever bug it never held had died decades ago. I told the agent that this was a very, very special family heirloom that my wife would miss dearly. They were to take the offending wood base off and salvage the remaining portion of the decoration. Which they begrudgingly did. Neither Cindy nor Lesley remembered the thing. Today the framed remainder of the decoration hangs in our home every holiday season. A fun reminder of the point I made.

Counterpoint: Customs repacking the container. The original tetras work by the packers in Singapore impossible to duplicate. When our container arrived at the house, it was followed by an open-bed truck with the items that didn't fit, including our fully unprotected mattress and box spring. And a packing job in the container itself that resulted in eleven either broken or missing items. Multiple times I was asked to sign-off on the shipment. Each time I asked to speak to management. Each time refused. Never did sign.

Chapter Seven

→ A Good Life in North Carolina

October 6, 2007: A little over ten years after moving to Singapore, it was wheels up to move out. To be frank, a very sad day for me. They say anywhere you live for more than seven years becomes your home. This had been the case. We had just lived a decade-long adventure, a different country almost every month for work, vacationing, or sporting events. The boy's educational school interim trips in high school saw them bike riding in Spain, abseiling in New Zealand, watching orangutans in Malaysia and exploring in Bali, to name a few. We all made great, interesting friends along the way, now scattered all over the world. What was a very difficult decision—to move there in the first place—had evolved into the best decision of my life.

Life was to move on in North Carolina, in Wake Forest just north of Raleigh where Cindy's sister and brother-in-law lived. We bought a home there, and I made a complete flip in careers, going from consumer bank training to executive recruiting in the sporting goods business. In 2003 we had purchased what would turn out to be our second home, a beach cottage in Sunset Beach at the southern tip of North Carolina. A bit on the small side, it had been our home base while in Singapore and we now rented it during the vacation season. Just as we were gathering a bit of momentum in the new life, the economic downturn of 2009 struck. Times two houses. And working in an industry where clients suddenly didn't need to pay you to help them not hire people. That was the downside. But there were more than offsetting upsides.

Both boys lived with us at different times while between jobs for 3-6 months each. For most families that development is not necessarily the greatest of news. But for us it was terrific, as we had spent all of their college years half of a world away, seeing them at most twice per year. Reconnecting was very rewarding. And it didn't hurt that friends in our new neighborhood had a son who would introduce Kyle to the woman who would eventually become a part of the family, Leigh, marrying Kyle in 2014. Can't put a price tag on that development. They would show us miracles, discussed in a later section of this book.

Before that happy time, and in a strange twist of fate, both boys would end up working in Raleigh and share an apartment. They declared simultaneously that their careers needed a boost, so decided to return to graduate school. Corey to become a lawyer and Kyle to improve his journalistic skills with a top school in that field. After a lengthy selection and application process, Corey chose DePaul Law School, and Kyle Northwestern's Journalism program. Both in Chicago. So they picked up their Raleigh apartment and moved to Wrigleyville together. Two die hard Cardinals fans living a block away from the rival Cubs stadium.

Meanwhile back at the Rod Ranch, the good Lord smiled on us just as things were getting tough economically. An old friend from Singapore who had repatriated to his home in London and was now working for Barclays called. He asked if I could help him with installation of Collections and Fraud Management training at his bank. I replied that I didn't have much else to do at the moment, sat down to come up with a company name (Level Four International, for the four levels of training effectiveness) and a logo (I doodle in arrows for some reason, so four arrows became the brand) and went to work designing courses and adding simulations written by the same developer I had used for decades before. Cindy set up the company and we were in business. Funny how things work out.

Golfing Charm

For anyone who plays this silly game, using golf and charm in the same sentence can be a rarity. I will always remember the first time playing with Cindy's last stepfather, when on the first tee he asked how long I had been playing golf. When I replied about 30 years, his retort was "I've been playing this game for 63 years and haven't enjoyed a minute of it." Three minutes in particular are worth mention here.

In Wake Forest we lived on the Heritage Golf Club and new friend Treavor and I regularly played golf there. He was relatively new to the game, working on his skills relentlessly. One day we were playing a twosome, both poorly, he had pulled out an old beat up ball, and we teed off at the par three 136 yard 12th hole, all carry over water. His shot was perfect, landing just off the fringe and rolled into the cup for his first hole in one. The celebration brought a neighbor from two houses away. I advised Treavor that the golfer with a hole in one traditionally was responsible for the bar tab. He happily agreed and in the nineteenth hole we started in on scotch, calling the wives and letting them know that we would be taking them out to dinner at the club later. Later came, we had not left the bar and the next call had us asking for a ride home. Cindy would say that she knew by the sound of my voice on the first call that there wasn't going to be a dinner for them.

Fast forward a couple of years, and I am paired up with my brother Al in Santa Fe at this member guest tournament. In the opening shoot-out, he knocked in a 110 yard sand wedge for his first hole in one. Oddly he had had five double eagles (a score of two on a par 5) from distances ranging 180-220 yards in his lifetime.

Fast forward another couple of years, and playing again in a twosome with my brother-in-law Joe. The 150-yard eighth hole at Thistle Cameron at Sunset Beach, and he hit a perfect shot that rolled in for, you guessed it, his first hole in one.

I've never had one. But I do hire out.

St. Andrews

While we are on golf, I would be remiss without mentioning my golfing trip of a lifetime, to the home of golf at St. Andrews. This should be a bucket list item for any gofer with a soul. When you stand on the first tee of the Old Course, if you don't feel something special then you are dead inside.

Our trip was in 2010, a week after The Open was played there. They were still taking the grandstands down when we arrived. My brother and two friends from Santa Fe filled out the foursome. We played The New Course, Jubilee, The Old Course, Carnoustie (Car*nastie* to be sure) and my personal favorite, Kingsbarns. Before the trip I hatched an idea to wear plus four (knickers) outfits on the Old Course. Which my brother and friends poo pooed. Then a couple of weeks later they came around to the idea. So now we're behaving like old women asking each other what colors each outfit will be. We settled on four different combinations. To my surprise there were few players so attired, and we were the only full foursome that day with plus fours. Made for a very cool picture on the bridge at 18.

Having lived in Singapore for ten years, I was the only one skilled at right hand drive cars, a welcome relief for my cohorts. One of them tried to drive and we quickly dismissed the idea as a bad one. The other two didn't bother.

Our caddies were terrific each day, with one of the crews signing on two rounds in succession, and joining us for a pint after the final round. They were very necessary to the enjoyment of the golf. On one occasion I had a fifty-foot putt, and my caddie said "right edge." I looked at him and said, "who do you think you're caddying for?" To which he replied, "hit it at the hole." On eighteen I was in the valley of sin, a very deep swale in the front of the green. He handed me my putter, pointed out the line and said "you're going to be short." I thought to myself, I'll show him and bashed that putt as hard as I could. Twelve feet short. Made the putt for par to applause of a few bystanders and tipped my flat cap to them. One of the most special times on a golf course. Ever.

I mentioned Kingsbarns. Referred to as the Pebble Beach of Scotland, you can see the ocean from most of the holes. We played 27 holes there on the last of our five days, and had a bit of rain for two holes, the only rain we had experienced all week. Rare for that trip and probably the reason I won't go back. The chances of being that lucky twice are slim.

We stayed in town, spent our non-golfing hours wandering the shops and pubs, participating in an (educational) scotch tasting, and enjoyed each other's company. Doesn't get much better.

Kyle and Leigh Wedding

I mentioned earlier in this work that moving into a certain neighborhood in Wake Forest, NC resulted in friendships that would eventually bring together our son Kyle and daughter-in-law Leigh. They were terrific together from the start, and had a wedding for the ages.

The venue was in the foothills of North Carolina outside of Asheville, at a remote retreat that featured a 5,000 square foot deck on the main guest house as well as satellite cabins. There was ample room to house the immediate families as well as the wedding parties. Below the deck was a firepit and charming babbling brook. Guests were bussed from a nearby hotel.

The entire event was largely home spun. While food was catered and a large tent covering the deck was rented, virtually everything else had unique, personal touches. Bride-to-be Leigh unleashed her unique creativity on homemade guest gifts, games, photo 'booth' and other elegant touches. The groom requested homemade beer, and a double hopped IPA was brewed by yours truly. The 48 bottles would disappear rather quickly at the main event. Also brewed was good old-fashioned Red Eye, a German recipe that has withstood decades leading back to well before my time on this earth. It's essentially browned white sugar, water and Everclear (grain alcohol), plus a few touches that will not be published here. Growing up in North Dakota, weddings were frequented by red eye bottles toted around the perimeter of the dance floor (polkas galore) all night with single shot glasses that everyone shared. No worries on this front, red eye killed any germs in the area code. I purposely made this batch quite light on alcohol, as I correctly anticipated many toasts. The wedding theme was a logo depicting a bride tackling a rugby player (both son's passion) who was dressed from the waist up in a tuxedo on top and rugby shorts below the waist. This same logo would adorn the red eye bottles, shot glasses (for all participants this time), and can/bottle cozies. And the logo would become more real than we imagined as the dancing began.

    Set up was a family and friends affair. Leigh's brother Robert had a U-Haul packed full of paraphernalia, signature item being the metal arch he made for the bride and groom to stand under at the ceremony. Which looked exactly like a set of grape vines. We turned on some tunes, set up tables, hung speakers, arranged the favors, got to know each other in the process and generally had a great time. Except for bride who hurt her ankle early in the day and would be in a walking boot for the wedding. She handled it like a trooper.

    At most nuptials, there is a wedding and a party breaks out. With family and wedding party staying onsite at this remote location, we had a three-day party where a wedding broke out. It was a fantastic weekend.

The ceremony was touching, relaxed and funny all at the same time, a true representation of the wonderful relationship between Kyle and Leigh. They make each other laugh. Attendees numbered just under 100, an eclectic mix of family, friends, rugby mates and Singapore connections. Some were a little touched (specific stories reserved for the moment).

Following the ceremony, a bit of speechifying included Corey hitting a home run on the best man effort. During which we learned for the first time about a couple of 'transgressions' that the boys were able to pull over on Mom and Dad undetected.

The post ceremony was accentuated by a couple of traditional holdovers from my past. First the flower eating. Which I had partaken in at numerous weddings. So (bride approved) we, the wedding party chowed down here as well. Then the obligatory Red Eye Toast. And of course (to a few) the all-important shoe toast. In my early days, our aforementioned third baseman had a proclivity to drink out of his (or sadly other's) shoes postgame at our sponsor's bar. Which turned into a shoe toast led by him at Cindy and my wedding. Seemed rude not to carry this forward, particularly given the natural match to the rugby tradition of 'shooting the boot.'

Ceremony and post shenanigans now complete it was time to party and dance. The rugby contingent disappeared around the corner just long enough to remove their pants and return with their respective team shorts and socks. (Also bride approved). The Singapore contingent gathered for a picture with Kyle supplied Tiger beers. And the party was epic, culminating at the fire pit by the stream below.

Another fantastic small world story broke out at the wedding. Class and teammate Sean from the Singapore days approached Cindy to ask if our niece Ali, "the pretty blond one", was dating anyone and if he could ask her out. Cindy replied, "Sean, Kyle and Corey really love their cousin, so if you hurt her, they'll hurt you bad." He was fine with the warning, they soon became inseparable and today are married with two kids. Sean's dad had been a baseball and football coach (in the football league I commissioned) while in Singapore, and our boys played on numerous teams with and against Sean. Surrealistic to be sure.

Finally, Uncle Joe and Aunt Lesley hosted a great brunch the day after the wedding. Sadly some of the champagne that was earmarked for the brunch was (accidentally) discovered at the post party the evening before. Not a well-received gesture by the ruggers and Corey took the hit for that one.

"Never do anything just right." This saying was etched on the beer glass given to me by the bride and groom. Cindy's gift brought her to tears. A ceramic jewelry container that said "Thank you for raising the man of my dreams."

Miracle Family of Three

We're all here for a reason and I am so looking forward to seeing this family story play out. It involves oldest son Kyle, wife Leigh and son Locke. Let's begin by saying that there is a happy ending for all three. Which as you are about to read could have been many combinations of a different story.

It begins with Leigh, and given that she will heavily redact this portion I'll be brief at the start. One of the happier days in our lives was a February 2017 phone call from Kyle telling us that they were pregnant with a boy. Due date in late October. We were overjoyed. The pregnancy took more than one difficult turn, the details of which are not important now but the short story included blood pressure issues and three hospital stays, the last of which culminated in our grandson being born on eclipse day, August 21, 2017. Nine weeks early, he was all of 3 lbs. 6 oz. We rushed from Sunset Beach to Alexandria to see him and help as we could. When Kyle took me into NICU to see Locke, I looked at that little bundle of more wraps and wires than boy and saw his little back double pumping on each hard-earned breath. First thing I told Kyle was "He's a fighter. *He's going to be alright.*" Forty days in NICU, and he was finally taken home. Today he is a regulation toddler, 25 lbs. by his second birthday, now four years old and along with his little sister Carter, joys of our lives. Inside of a few months the same hospital saved the lives of our daughter-in-law and grandson.

The hospital's job wasn't done. What follows is the ordeal that Kyle went through a short nine months later, Memorial Day weekend 2018, described in my initial Caring Bridge description:

"This is a tough time for Kyle. Last week he had a case of strep throat that appeared to be getting better, when he took a sudden turn for the worse on Sunday, May 27. By Monday he had developed what appeared to be bacterial

meningitis. He has been in the ICU since that time, and was largely unresponsive for the first four days. He was intubated to help him breath and process oxygen. Then there was the waiting game for cultures, which can be compromised by the fact that he was on antibiotics prior to the main event. There were also counter intuitive symptoms which complicated the diagnosis, and he also developed pneumonia and another viral infection in the lungs. Throughout his vitals have been good, labs good and as you know he is a horse who will fight these little invaders. His wife Leigh has been by his side every possible minute. Mom, Dad and Corey as well as mother-in-law Ann are in Alexandria with him to stay by his side and help with Kyle and Leigh's 9 month-old son Locke. Corey received a welcome mini-rise out of his older brother early on with a typically Jahner jab.

We will continue to use this site to keep you updated on his condition. Feel free to pass along your thoughts which will be read to Kyle when he is ready. Prayers, well wishes and love have flowed in from around the world, and mean the world to all of us."

The Memorial Day drive from Sunset Beach to DC in a pouring rain, cramming a six-hour drive into nine was the longest of our lives. Upon arrival Kyle was gasping for every breath and in the process of being transferred to the very hospital that had saved Leigh and Locke. I wore my father's rosary out, held it on Kyles shoulder, and asked God not to take our son. Cindy felt the hands of both of his grandfathers on her shoulder, literally, in support. On morning two of the longest four days of our lives while he was in a coma, I heard a voice as clear as someone standing in the room saying just five words. *"He's going to be alright."* A sense of calm washed over me, and I knew in my soul that it was the voice of God himself. Between those words and Locke's smiles we got through it.

Two mornings later, Kyle in his fourth day of coma, Cindy asked me as I was getting ready to go to the hospital "Did He (God) give you a timeframe?" I said no, that I'd ask but He was no doubt a little busy with others.

When Kyle finally awoke, there were other disturbing symptoms, paralysis at the top of the list, that were unexplained. For those of you who have ever watched the medical mystery TV show House, what played out at the foot of his bed was like an episode of that series. Four doctors trying to figure out what was going on. More tests, and the realization that on top of meningitis, he also had transverse myelitis affecting the spine. So when he could finally send signals to his body, the myelitis blocked them. I won't bore you with the details posted daily on his website, but over time he began to be himself again, getting past many disturbing transitions, and eventually earning a transfer to a third hospital for cognitive, speech and physical therapies. People we knew were having people we didn't know take to their knees to pray for him. There were over 2,500 visits to his site. Our beliefs were further strengthened. And thirty days to the day of becoming ill, he was home feeding his son.

After a couple of weeks of working out with Kyle at home (for a fleeting moment I could do as many push-ups as he) he strengthened by the minute. Six months later he was playing rugby again. His last entry in the Caring Bridge site follows:

"Hello everyone who is for some reason still checking this site. Kyle here; just wanted to say how grateful for all the support and well-wishing I am, much of it before I could even realize the gravity of the situation. Thanks to Dad setting this up to keep you all informed with no effort on my part. I figured I'd close it down with a note thanking you and summarizing the experience, two weeks removed from four weeks in three hospitals.

Luckily (for me, anyway) I didn't really have to worry the way others did. I don't remember going to the ER with a massive headache, convincing a practitioner and Leigh I felt better and could go home, failing to respond the next day, two ambulance rides, nor two lumbar punctures plus many other medical interventions. Really the next few days didn't exist for me; even when I indicated consciousness my ability to log long-term memories was out of order, and only started coming back in spurts near the very end of intubation.

Before this I knew nearly nothing of meningitis and literally nothing about transverse myelitis. You all knew I had it before I did. When I did come around, I was actually kinda stupid and irritating [insert joke here], but slowly my infected brain got better and I became more and more myself. Days later, once a half-competent, big-picture cognition returned, my wife explained how tenuous and serious it had all been, which I guess made sense since even then I could barely move most of my body.

The next few weeks both flew and took forever. They felt long, involving worries I'd never be quite right as I'd never been unable to do some of these things and learned not all recover. But given where I was when I awoke, my body and mind recovered far more rapidly than anyone could reasonably expect. I'm forever impressed by people who have to deal with the kind of limitations so temporarily laid on me. Many struggle much harder and longer, some for the rest of their lives. No pity for Kyle; this was a crazy irritant but big picture there's so much worse out there. I was a little wobbly when I went home, but now I am already feeling close to (a very out of shape version of) my old self, with few lingering minor issues.

So, again, thank you all for the support and good vibes, sorry if I scared you and glad this had a happy ending. I'm incredibly lucky (except for the whole contracting-this-bizarre-thing part) because of incredible wife (especially), family and friends, and a mind-boggling dose of modern medicine. Hospital visits including Corey's flight from Chicago, various texts, cards, reading materials for the hospital, a signed rugby ball from my team, meals for the family...it was all overwhelming and greatly appreciated. Now stop worrying about me if you haven't already and have a great week."

You too, Kyle. And Leigh. And Locke. Lots of them.

Before moving on, a special shout out to the nurses and doctors in three different INOVA hospital locations in the DC area, with Fairfax on the top of the list, particularly in NICU. And to Medicare for swooping in on expenses that would break any young family. And to the March of Dimes for their continuing great work raising awareness and funds for premature babies. We could all expound on these great organizations at length.

A Scissors story

I had been having my hair cut by a woman named Candy for a number of years, and told her that one of these days I would bring in the barber shears that my dad used about a half century ago. I had kept them safe all those years, moving from home to home and continent to continent. One well-travelled pair of scissors.

I finally remembered to take them to the stylist, who immediately recognized them as very high quality and still very sharp. I asked if she would like to cut my hair with them. Candy, a bit surprised and touched, said that she absolutely would like to do so. She showed the shears to her stylist Michelle who looked at them and exclaimed, "He was a lefty." Which was true. Candy cut my hair as usual and for the first time in years she finished by parting my hair on the right side, opposite of normal. I waited until she was done and told her, "Candy, you have never parted my hair on the wrong side before. Dad is here." To which Michelle went wall-to-wall goose bumps. Great moment.

So, we made it a routine, and I am the only customer who brings his own scissors. A few cuts into this new protocol, Candy said she would oil the scissors to keep them in good shape. She then asked when I had done so, as there was fresh oil on the hinge. I have never put a drop of oil on those scissors, and they have never been in the possession of anyone else. More goosebumps. I'm not sure Candy nor Michelle are ever going to be the same. Thankfully they were a little different to begin with anyway...

Stents for the Memories

When you have chest pains, go to the hospital. Seems like reasonable advice. Couldn't tell by this genius. In September of 2018 I was working in the yard on a hot day and felt a pain that ran the length of my sternum. Sat down, had some Gatorade, and it went away. I continued working and it happened again. More rest, more Gatorade, and finish the job. I'm thinking, 'I'm out of shape, haven't worked-out much on the heels of Kyle's recent illness, and it's a hot humid day. This will pass. And I have a physical scheduled next month if anything persists.'

My tipping point was carrying a case of wine up a flight of stairs. Sternum on fire. OK, this I can't live with. The wine part I mean.

I mentioned the issue to my general practitioner, who immediately placed me on a stress test. Which I apparently flunked, so was sent to a cardiac specialist. A week later I was on the table getting a few new parts. Four stents. Turns out that I had an 89% blockage in the 'widow maker' and another 78% block in a different fork in the artery road. The whole procedure was done through my wrist, while awake (on some you-won't-care-about-anything joy juice), and able to watch my heart beating on a 70 inch flat screen. At one point I saw the balloon expand while a stent was being inserted. Fascinating stuff. In the hospital for twenty-four hours, didn't realize until after how bad I felt by comparison and was back in the office a couple days later.

Wake-up call complete, I participated in 36 cardiac rehab sessions, drastically changed my diet, dropped 25 lbs. and did not improve my golf game one iota. Mostly good news.

Then came family extensions, also with happy endings. Brother Al called to thank me for waking him up to the reality of our family history and summarily flunked his calcium test. He went through the same exploratory procedure that resulted in my stents, only to find nothing wrong. Brother-in-law Joe flunked a stress test and also went through the procedure, again to find that there was nothing wrong with his heart. I was so looking forward to holding the 'I saved your lives' thing over the both of them for the rest of their days on this Earth. Instead I end up with the two of them plotting what to do to me for putting them through the procedure.

Life is not fair.

Chapter Eight

→ Gone to a Better Life

It goes without saying that my parents top this list. They have more significant roles in this work, so no need to repeat here. Suffice to say that praying Dad's rosary and lighting Mom's candle have brought me serenity in the most trying of times. The great ones never really leave us, and to this day, in the year that Dad passed a half century ago and Mom already ten years gone, I still feel their watchful eyes.

The same goes for stepfather, Walt, who treated all of us like kings and queens after marrying Mom and celebrating 31 years together.

On the following pages are some very special people in my life, stepbrother Gene, former roommates Bruce and Pat who stood up for me at our wedding, a great boss Carl, golfing buddy Craig and most recently mentor Gene, the inspiration for a foundation that will help thousands of kids through the game of golf. All were the sources of great stories, some of which are shared here. The order is family first, then chronologically as they became major influences on my life.

Gene Bartholome
August 24, 1943 - May 23, 2002

Gene was my stepbrother through the marriage of Mom to Walter Bartholome, spoken of earlier. This is taken from his obituary:

"Gene enjoyed many activities over the years, including motorcycle racing and touring, cross-country skiing and hiking. He enjoyed fishing and became an avid golfer. He was keenly interested in history, was a voracious reader and took pleasure in music and working on his computer. He was gregarious and loved helping people; his wry wit and warm sense of humor will be greatly missed by the many friends with whom he shared his interests."

Quite frankly the words do not do the man justice. He was first and foremost, his own man and a free spirit. He treated me as if I were his natural brother in spite of a ten-year gap in age, significant at the time of our families uniting. His parties were epic and he had a stereo that was top notch. Before then I had never seen a cassette player with a window on top revealing a mechanical arm that would reach in, pull the cassette out, flip it over and reinsert it back to play the second side. Unique and quintessentially Gene.
    There was a rumor at one point that Gene's stereo was on a theft list. As the story goes, he and a friend who worked at the local zoo brought an adult female mountain lion to his house, placed it in the living room beside the stereo and

went out for the night. Not sure if anyone attempted entry, but there would have been a laundry problem if they had.

I remember his dad Walter and I bringing food to Gene on the occasion of his Penton motorcycle unfortunately falling on his chest in a motocross race. He was not in good shape that day, and would shortly thereafter convert to the less demanding enduro racing style, no doubt a bit later than the decision should have been made.

Gene passed away suddenly from heart failure. We lived in Singapore at the time. Less than two months before I had made the trip from a baseball tournament in Perth, Australia to Bismarck, ND for his dad Walter's funeral. Back in Singapore, my brother Al called one morning while I was driving to work. He seldom called me as his international dialing rates were huge as compared to mine, so I flippantly asked him, "Who died?" He responded "Gene." It took a minute or two for him to convince me that he was not kidding. To this day I have not used that line again. Although from above I'm sure Gene thought it was hysterical.

Back in Bismarck for the funeral and celebration of his life, it became quickly apparent that Gene's internment would be unlike most others. Check that, all others. His favorite beer by a long shot was Budweiser in long neck bottles and his wine of choice was Chianti. Gene had traveled far and wide over the years on motorcycle, cross country skiing and golfing trips, and friends from many of his favorite haunts were present. He had been cremated and wife Sue had portioned out parts of him into, you may have guessed it, Budweiser bottles with Chianti cork stoppers. Friends were taking him back to his many homes away from home. I asked Sue if she thought he would like to travel to Asia and, surprised at the offer she said absolutely. So I packed one of those Bud bottles with part of my stepbrother into my bag and transported him back to Singapore. Not exactly legal, but the primary objective was achieved. His love for golf had blossomed later in life than most, so I sprinkled parts of him on golf courses in Singapore, Malaysia and Indonesia. The remainder would be (discretely) dropped into the bay in Singapore which my office overlooked. The chosen receptacle needed to be better sealed and more locally appropriate, so I chose a Royal Selangor pewter drink flask with golf ball dimple design, highly stylish yet functional. Which conveniently came equipped with a small funnel. I glanced up at my reflection in the mirror of my master bathroom while pouring my stepbrother's ashes from a beer bottle into that flask through the funnel and thought to myself, "my life has now changed in a way I did not see coming."

When this world ends the good Lord is going to have one hell of a time putting Gene back together.

I am thankful for the many stories, laughs, rounds of golf and especially that Walter did not live to bury his son.

Rest in peace my brother.

Bruce Lohstreter
April 8, 1952 - January 3, 2016

I met Bruce when I was a freshman in college, and we were best of friends from the start. He grew up on a dairy farm and we just so happened to be dating two best friends in Mary and Kathy. Bruce and I probably drank too much in those days. No, check that, we definitely drank too much. Bruce was a girl magnet. He had scary good looks, laughed from the ankles and was one of the most genuine people I ever knew. He and Kathy would eventually marry, have four wonderful kids and sadly divorce when the kids were grown. Both remarried, and a heart attack took Bruce from us when he was only 63, ironically the same age that my dad was when he passed.

We roomed together in college, living off campus at the University of North Dakota in Grand Forks. As juniors the two of us shared an apartment, and frequented Frenchy's, the local college bar. We discovered foosball together, getting our butts kicked when we started playing. Then we found a dumpy little place, often deserted but with a foosball table. There we would practice for hours, one-on-one and doing setups where I worked on my shooting skills and he in his goalie role. Then back to Frenchy's, placing a quarter on the table to challenge, and get beat again, by a little less. Back to the other place for more practice. Over time we became good at the game, and other teams were the ones leaving the table in defeat. It was a blast.

Our apartment had one designated parking spot with an outlet that was activated inside so a car could be plugged in so it would start in the cold winters. Grand Forks routinely duked it out with International Falls, Minnesota for the coldest spot in the nation. Worst day I remember was 32 degrees below zero with a wind chill of minus 90. We went to school like any other day. I plugged my car in via a 50-foot extension cord running out of a window in our living room. Morning routine was to get up, activate the soft plug heaters on our car engines from inside the apartment, shower and by that time the cars would start. We both drove Plymouth Barracudas. Mine was a '65 with a sloping back window and fold down seats and trunk divider that created enough space to slide my waterbed parts in for moving. His was a slick looking '67 coupe. When it's below zero, those plastic seats in my 'Cuda were like sitting on cold concrete. By the time I reached school in fifteen minutes or so, the car was just getting comfortably warm, the seat a bit softened and it was time to get out. We all carried jumper cables. Pretty much everyone over the age of four in North Dakota knows how to jump-start a car with a dead battery.

When we moved back to our parent's homes in Bismarck/Mandan, Bruce brought a large truck to school, 270 miles away. In our 'Cudas we could make that drive in just over three hours. Speed limits were 75 and there were very few cars on the divided highways. A little slower in the truck. We packed it, and tied down a large tarp that covered the open box. The tarp was secured the way Bruce was taught. It was a windy day and halfway home that tarp ripped from front to back. When we finally arrived at the Lohstreter farm that evening, the exchange between Bruce and his dad was epic. "You didn't tie the (expletive) thing down right" was the beginning of a back and forth that used every swear word in the book. I wasn't so much surprised by any particular words, but I will say that the order was impressive.

In our senior year, we rented a three-bedroom house with Pat O'Brien, another great friend who sadly is in this chapter as well. We needed a couch, so Bruce and Pat went thrift store shopping while I was busy assembling the wood plank and cement block, highly stylish yet functional, stereo and TV shelf in the living room. They returned with a ratty couch, the back of which conveniently folded down converting it into a bed for that extra guest who needed a place to crash. Nice feature. I asked how much the seller wanted. $25. I asked how much they paid. $25. They were surprised when I suggested that they could have offered less for this piece of, let me think, furniture. We put it in place and fold it down for testing. Bruce lies down and rolls over, at which point the entire couch flips on its side, throwing him onto the floor. Now we have free entertainment. Whenever we had a guest, we proudly folded that baby down, showed them their comfy bed, retired to our rooms and waited for the inevitable scream when the couch did its work. Best 25 bucks we ever spent.

It seemed whenever I drove somewhere and Bruce was riding with me, no matter how crowded a parking lot, there was a space available not only in the front row, but the front spot. It drove him crazy, considering when he drove, we were just about better off leaving his car at home vs. taking the parking spot left for him. When I flew out of Myrtle Beach for his funeral, the very front spot was available for me, something that had never come close to happening in many trips before. And one of his favorite songs was playing on the radio as I pulled in. He was there with me and as I thanked him, I could imagine him laughing from those ankles again.

Pat O'Brien
January 24, 1953 - September 5, 2015

Pat was a friend in grade school, coming from a family of successful wrestlers. My first foray into the sport was in seventh grade, and as mentioned earlier, I had the misfortune of being in the same weight class. He would go on to become a very successful high school wrestler, as well as football player, and often recreated hunting and fishing. We roomed together for a year in college, and after school for a time. There was always something to laugh at with Pat.

Minot County Jail. This is more about me than Pat, although I maintain that if he had not won the state wrestling championship his senior year, I may not have celebrated as vigorously, and perhaps would not have had the company of those nice felons in jail for an evening of rest and relaxation.

The Beetle. At the University of North Dakota Pat owned a Volkswagen Beetle, the most valuable part of which was the two mag wheels on the back. The car had no brakes other than the emergency hand brake. He gave me a ride to school one day and as always needed his coffee (glass mug, no sippy cup for him) and smoked Vantage cigarettes (who smoked those things anyway? I was a smoker and couldn't stand the smell of them). So, on this drive he was steering, shifting gears, using the hand brake to stop, smoking his cigarette and drinking his coffee. Never missed a beat. It was poetry in motion to watch.

Wake Up Call. Grand Forks, senior year, Bruce, Pat and I living together. Pat had a very small bedroom, and was a notorious sleeper. He had two old fashioned alarm clocks, the clanging ones, perched on metal TV trays for extra noise. And routinely slept through the racket. He told me one day that he needed help getting up for a test that could not be missed. Alarm clocks go off, trays shake, people across town hear it and get up. Pat sleeps like a baby. So I entered the room and began to shake him. At which point, still half asleep, he takes a cut at me. Nice little round house hook that misses my nose by inches. Round two is now over, Pat still dozing. Round three, I opened his window (it was about 20 degrees outside), grabbed his covers, ran out of the room and closed the door. Very effective. Can still hear him screaming those new names for me. He never asked me to wake him up again.

Typing Leases. After college, Pat and I lived together in Bismarck when he was starting out in the oil business. At least six months of six days a week, driving 100 miles out to the Dickinson area to source leases, then typing them up back home in the evening. On most nights as I went to bed, he was typing with two fingers. The leases needed to be perfect, with no white-out and word processing software was not a thing yet. So if a mistake was made, the process started over. I can't count the number of times that I heard plink, plink, plink.....godammit....and then the *zzzzzzz* as the paper flew out of the typewriter. Every morning there would be a pile of crumpled paper in the corner of the kitchen, the remains of a wrong plink.

Pat passed away due to complications from rheumatoid arthritis, which he battled for the better part of forty years, having endured about as many surgeries. And he never complained. It's the 'hand he was dealt' he would say. Quite an inspiration to say the least.

Both Bruce and Pat were groomsmen at my wedding. Rest in peace my friends.

Carl Main
July 14, 1943 - February 12, 2016

I worked for Carl in consumer banking. He was more than a boss as we became friends, golfing buddies and were occasionally inappropriate in chasing a laugh. When I heard the sad news of Carl's passing a flood of great memories came back.

Work and Play. We met at a small subsidiary of Citibank, which had considerable problems with loan quality. Carl was brought in to manage the collections department, and I was on a project team to help organize that activity. After the project I went to work directly for Carl. He took delight in scheduling his interviews with the sun at his back, blinds wide open and the statue of a vulture on the windowsill placed strategically over his shoulder. So, to look at him, you were also staring at a vulture in the middle of the sun. If you asked to close the blinds, or shifted your assigned seat, you had a better opportunity to be hired. Timid was not a good trait when it came to the man. We laughed many times about that technique.

Play Gone Wrong. Same business, one day the CEO (his boss) was traveling, and Carl was in his office with a peer. Next thing you knew paramedics were carting Carl out of the office on a stretcher, white as a sheet. We assumed the worst, only to find out that he and Dave had been arm wrestling, resulting in Carl's upper arm breaking into a spiral fracture. Upon return to the office in the cast, my new job was to help him tie his tie in the morning. He would soon fire me from that task finding that he could use his teeth as effectively as my assistance.

And The Winner Is...The first round of golf I played with Carl began with my comment that I'd better make sure that the boss wins. I can still hear him say, "Out here we are equals. If I catch you not doing your best to beat me I'll fire you on the spot." And that's the way it stayed. Tough but fair in the office, all fun and games once we left the confines.

What Are The Odds? One benefit golf tournament is particularly memorable. We played in Southeast Denver, the course escapes me now but one of Carl's tee shots never will. There was a power wire about 50 yards out from an elevated tee box, running straight across the fairway. By now you can see this coming—Carl's drive hit that power line flush, and the ball rebounded straight back at him, landing at the base of the tee box not 10 yards away from his feet. "Did you see that?" I had, and also had a hard time hitting my own drive after falling down laughing.

Golf in Phoenix. On a business trip it was mandatory to play golf. This particular day in Phoenix the temperature was 115 degrees. There were about three groups of crazies on the golf course. Carl and I played as a twosome in about 2½ hours. Never drank so much Gatorade in my life. That dry heat thing? Sorry, 115 is just plain hot. One guy made the turn between nines looking a little pink. Well, a lot pink. His friends told him to put on sunscreen, advice he declined. Last I heard at the end of the round he couldn't bend his burned legs to get out of the cart and was transported to the emergency room. You cannot fix stupid.

Our Wedding. Carl attended Cindy and my wedding in 1982. One of the more memorable moments was the shoe toast at our reception which was heartily joined by every male in the room, including Carl. I can still see him dumping his drink into his shoe, dipping it into the toe (as suggested by the 'gentleman' from my softball team leading the toast) and downing it out of the heel. I'm sure he had not done so before that day, and doubt ever after.

Wedding Crashing. Until our wedding I had no idea that Carl was a wedding crasher. After our reception he demonstrated that skill at not one but two other receptions in the same facility. As would be told later he had found out at one of the receptions that the bride was a Continental Airlines stewardess, and had also convinced the mother of the bride that he knew her quite well. He had never laid eyes on the young lady. Eventually one of the family members figured it out and asked him to crash someone else's wedding. Which he promptly did. All in good sport to Carl.

Dinner at The Overlook. Cindy and I honeymooned at Hilton Head, which was one of Carl's favorite places. He issued two orders. To take Cindy to the bar overlooking the 18th hole and Calibogue Sound at the Harbor Town Golf Links. Which we did. "You will say that it doesn't get any better than this" he said. He was right. The other directive was to take Cindy to dinner at The Overlook, one of his all-time favorite restaurants. On him. Just show up and everything would be taken care of. We enjoyed the evening, and dinner of a lifetime. I would (much) later tell him that the food was so good that neither of us minded the day of food poisoning that followed. Apparently, we were somewhat allergic to lobster bisque. Oh well....

Wine Offering. It would be many, many years later, around 2010 that I could return the restaurant favor properly. Not the food poisoning part, just the good restaurant part. Cindy and I had visited Paris and discovered a small restaurant named Le Relais de Venise. Relying upon our recommendation he took his girlfriend there. Not sure if he was just being nice but Carl would later tell me that it was now their "second favorite restaurant in Paris," high praise as he had traveled there regularly to visit his girlfriend for the better part of 20 years. He also said that he had a little surprise for us. A few days later a bottle of that wonderful table wine from the very same restaurant showed up on my doorstep in North Carolina. He had brought it back to Houston and shipped it to us. How classy is that? We enjoyed that bottle on a special occasion and were transported for a moment right back to Paris.

Carl Main. An amazing combination of drive, calmness, fun, good taste and thoughtfulness. Not necessarily in that order. Rest in Peace my friend. You have more than earned it.

Craig Kauffmann
November 24, 1946—April 17, 2012

When we lived in the Heritage golfing community in Wake Forest this gentleman moved in across the street. Friends Trevor, Jim and I found out that he was a divorced golfer and we asked him to join for a round. Halfway down the first fairway Craig and I were giving each other copious amounts of grief. That sealed it. We became a regular foursome for the next year and a half.

Craig was a great guy and a solid golfer. When in the service he played on the Army tennis team, and to this day I have yet to see anyone who was better centered and solid over a golf ball. I imagine all of that tennis was a contributor. He and Jim were the better golfers in the group, and often had a close match. That is until number 16, where for some reason Craig dialed-in and more often than not, edged Jim on the last three holes. We had great fun playing together.

At the age of 65 in 2012 Craig (we found out later) ignored some minor chest pains. It would prove to be a fatal mistake, one that I recalled when I had similar symptoms when I was also 65, and acted upon them. Had it not been for Craig I might not be writing this.

The sixteenth hole at Heritage now has a bench in his honor, with the inscription Kauffman's Korner. It's our tribute to a good friend at that turning-point in so many of his rounds. Rest in peace, and thank you Craig for being my inspiration to get better.

Gene Weldon
October 23, 1948 - January 13, 2017

Gene became a friend when we purchased a golf membership from him, the year we decided to move to Sunset Beach. As it so happened about two months after we started paying dues, the course was sold and new ownership cancelled all memberships. Down-payments all disappeared in the transaction. So my cost per round at that point was around $500. I never let him forget that one.

Gene was polite beyond polite, addressing all of us as "Sir." He is described in an excerpt from the website for a foundation that now bears his name:

"Gene Weldon was a near 50-year PGA Professional in the famous Carolinas section. He was an instrumental figure, alongside golf legend Carolyn Cudone, in the foundation and development of a formidable junior golf program in the Myrtle Beach area. Described by all who crossed his path as a true gentleman who would do anything to help a friend, Gene is sorely missed by many after losing a hard-fought battle to cancer in January of 2017. Gene's passion was youth golf but he didn't just teach children how to play the game. He taught them how to love it. He believed golf was a reflection of life and that life is about friendship and responsibility. Gene was a passionate supporter of The First Tee through a variety of innovative programs, tournaments and fundraising activities. He was the quintessential Southern Gentlemen, calling you sir and doing anything for you."

The foundation, Gene's Dream, was created by celebrity friends and those close to him in the Myrtle Beach area. In its first year of operation, the Gene's Dream Foundation wrote a $50,000 check to the First Tee of Coastal Carolinas. In the second, Liberty Mutual chose Gene's Dream to be a partner charity and the one to be featured in its annual charitable tournament, the largest of its kind. He would be so proud.

The website does so much more justice to the man than I could in a page or two. I urge you to take a browse at www.genesdream.com.

Most recently, Mr. Gene Weldon has, deservedly so, been accepted into the Myrtle Beach Golf Hall of Fame, with induction ceremonies scheduled for September, 2022.

Rest well, sir.

Chapter Nine

> → Life Lessons 101A:
> Airlines and Stupidity

I've spent a fair amount of time on airplanes in my life. Somewhere around 4 million miles thanks to a little back-of-the-envelope math. I actually prefer long flights, the longer the better really, as long as in business class.

Those of us who spent this much time aloft for business can recognize that 'look' from your seatmate at the beginning of a particularly long journey. Making eye contact and saying a pleasant hello, the 'look' says "you look like a nice person, now leave me alone while I enjoy one of the only remaining bits of time to myself, and we'll chat in the last half hour or so of this flight." Then you both shut up. This is therapy time.

As you might expect, so much travel will create some stories, a few highlights of which are shared on the following pages. There are more.

Qantas Times Two

Shortly after 9/11, I had occasion to fly Qantas to Sydney from Singapore for work. I always carry a Swiss Army pocketknife, the smallest one they make which provides a one-inch blade, small scissors, nail file and flat head screwdriver. Amazing how handy those little things can be. When departing Sydney, I forgot to place it into my checked suitcase, and it was confiscated by the TSA. Not sure what they thought an aging businessman was going to do with the thing, but such are the times. It wouldn't be the first one I would lose.

A couple hours later I was served dinner in the business class flight. I had chosen the steak, and the silverware placed in front of me included a serrated steak knife measuring about 4 inches long, fully capable of cutting my confiscated Swiss knife in half. I said to the stewardess, "You're kidding, right?" She replied that they had not quite rationalized their safety protocols yet. No kidding.

Another trip to Australia would be for a baseball tourney for the boys in Perth. Staying near the Margaret River wine region, we took the opportunity to tour the area and purchase wine for the return home. I carry a rolling briefcase for work and had it along this trip as well. At security, I'm told for the first time in, let me think, ever, that they must weigh my briefcase. "We at Qantas are very strict" was the reasoning. It was overweight, so I was told to check it. Which was not going to happen as it contained my most important files, pc and other electronics. My working life on wheels. So rather than check the bag I pulled some files and gave them to Cindy to put in her carry-on. Weighed again, still too heavy. The pc was next, going to one of the boys for in his carry-on. Security is watching this happen, and finally approved the weight of my briefcase, along with the weight of my family's carry-ons which contain the contents of the same briefcase. It gets better. The whole time this little drama is playing out, I have a duffle bag on my shoulder which I'm trying to make look light in weight. Which is a problem because it contains 11 bottles of wine and four bottles of local beer. The strap is almost cutting through my shoulder because that bag weighs twice as much as the overweight briefcase. It went right through. Almost threw my back out lifting it into the overhead storage on the plane.

Northwest Times Two

It used to be an art form to fly back to the states from Singapore. Around ten months before summer leave, the routine was to spend a couple of hours on the phone setting up flights, economy fares and frequent flyer miles upgrades to business class. It was worth the effort, as for 50,000 miles we were in business class across the pond, and first class for all domestic flights. Times four family members. And the airline gave us bonus-miles back as if we had purchased the business class tickets, 35,000 each. One year there was a promotion for flying across the Pacific in the summer, with a 20,000 bonus. So that year with the same routine, I bought four economy tickets, gave them 50,000 miles off of each of our accounts, and they gave us each back 55,000 miles. Small wonder they went broke and merged with Delta.

On a solo flight home one year, I was in the upper deck of a Boeing 747, a nice section of business class with four rows of four seats, two on each side. I was in the back row with a businesswoman beside me, and had placed my briefcase in a convenient, enclosed shelf behind the seat. The stewardess (one of three on the flight who were retiring after 30 years on NW Airlines, she being the angry one) opened the cabinet and asked "Who put this briefcase in here? On impact this will come right through!" My unfiltered mind answered "Who the hell do you think could have put it there? There are passengers and you up here." My filtered response was "I did, where would you like it moved?" Never further anger a flight attendant at the beginning of a 12-hour flight. That's a rule. When the episode was done my seatmate and I agreed that if this 747 went down, the location of my briefcase was going to be the least of our problems.

Sidebar, and interesting factoid. On Singapore air, the flight attendants are not allowed to be more than 30 years old. So these three NW honorees had been working on airplanes since before any Singapore Girl (that was how they were termed) had been born.

Upon arrival in Minneapolis, two carrousels were being used for the luggage return as there were around 400 bags to deal with. No worries, mine had the "Priority" tag on it, which most airlines return first. Not this time. After 30 minutes of watching the two streams of bags, I saw mine. And counted how many there were behind it. Nine. So much for priority.

Singapore Air

From clueless to disconcerting to stupid and back to reality. My favorite flight was direct from Newark to Singapore, 17-18 hours, in business class. Great decompression time, no pun intended. On one occasion we were about an hour out of Newark and ran into what seemed to be a pretty good storm. There were flashes of lighting and the plane shuddered through what felt like significant turbulence. Shortly thereafter, the pilot came on the speaker, saying "Some of you in the rear of the plane may have noticed that we had a little problem with one of our engines." Enter clueless and disconcerting part. There was no storm. The little problem was an engine on fire. They managed to put it out, and then the somewhat stupid part enters.

The next announcement was that they were in communication with the engineers to see if it was safe to proceed to Singapore with one less engine. As in two rather than the original three. We were now around 16 hours away. That was not going to happen. Instead, we flew over water for about 45 minutes dumping fuel and returned to Newark, stayed over-night and caught another flight the next morning.

The incident barely made the Straits Times newspaper in Singapore, commanding a page two column of about three inches. They chose not to advertise a problem with the number one airline on the planet.

Delta

This story isn't airline stupidity as much as it is my own. While living in Sunset Beach in 2018 I had a business trip that began with a week of work in Singapore, followed immediately by a week in Dallas. Both were training courses that require long days and by the end I was a bit tired. Adding to the tension was hurricane Florence which was bearing down on the Carolinas. Cindy had packed up the house and evacuated by car from Sunset Beach to Charlotte to stay with Cindy's niece Ali and husband Sean.

Conveniently, my flight home from Dallas connected through Charlotte, so the plan was to stop there and wait out the storm. I was tired so fell asleep on the plane and stayed in a near coma for the entire flight. I awoke on approach to the airport, and we had a smooth landing. Sean called and said there seemed to be a change in plans. I responded, no, I just landed in Charlotte. My seatmate then advised me that no, they had a mechanical on the flight and had returned to Dallas. I had no idea. He pulled up the itinerary on my phone and made a screen shot of it. DFW-DFW. I went into the airport and asked if they had a piece of equipment that had just a little more range.

There was another flight that night and we made Charlotte before the storm, so a happy ending. It was particularly happy for the wife of my seatmate who, at the baggage claim asked me if I was "that guy." I said yes and she had a little bit more than necessary laugh at my expense.

Chapter Ten

→ Life Lessons 101B:
Don't Do That

In the Introduction I spoke of the lists that helped me organize this work, so I thought I would end with—*let me think*—a list. You've all had miles and miles of email lists advising you on just about anything. Or just Google "Top Ten Lists" and as of this writing you'll have "About 968,000,000 results" at your fingertips - in 0.58 seconds. Thankfully I've done the work for you. I compared many such lists. I selected overlapping retrospective regrets from the learned, the not-so-learned, the elderly, the dying, CEOs looking back, passers-by-on-the-street, you name it. Really, no need to thank me. The fact of the matter is I try to do one nice thing every day, and I like to get it out of the way early.

From this extensive (okay, tens of minutes of) research, I created my own top-ten-or-so list of, not Do's like everyone else, but Don'ts. Not unlike my favorite golf lesson, given when a friend had a particularly bad shot. My sage advice, "Don't Do That."

So, here are the fruits of my thoughts, or if I could be so bold, advice. (I know, I'm a giver.)

Don't....

....work so hard. Susan Steiner, a palliative nurse and author of "The Top Five Regrets of the Dying" observed the top regret that surfaces over and over again, particularly from men, is the amount of time they worked. While not easy to change when you're trying to make a living, I can remember wearing long hours and frequent travel miles as a badge of honor. In retrospect they're really not. Work-life balance is what makes the modern executive really successful. Find an employer or passion that allows you and your kids to not be strangers. If they're not out of the house already, they will be sooner than you think.

....be so attached to social media, your phone, etc., etc. Take a hint from former executives of social media platforms who are not letting their own children set up an account, using reasons like "tremendous guilt," and "ripping apart the social fabric of how society works," and "no civil discourse, no cooperation, misinformation, mistruth." If your only interaction with other human beings is on a three-inch screen, you're not right. If you're driving back to the house for your forgotten phone when you're scheduled to be away for about ten minutes, stop it. And for God's sake, it's not a necessary element of your trip to the bathroom. Unplug once in a while. You'll live.

....forget to be kind. I joke about doing just one nice thing per day, and it is just that, a joke. Notice the random acts of kindness around you and create your own. Someone ahead of me at Subway paid for my lunch, and it made my day. I did the same at McDonalds and it felt great to know I was giving someone I'd never met a future heart attack. Smile, it's not that hard. Hold a door for a stranger. Let that car merge in front of you and wave thanks when someone does the same for you. Buy flowers for someone for no reason. And read everything written by Marc de Celle on the topic of Kindness. You'll be entertained, gather ideas and just might be a better person.

....lose touch with your friends. Glen and I grew up together from the second grade forward, and since moving out of Bismarck have called each other on our birthdays every year, for more years (ok, decades) that either of us is now comfortable to admit. I look forward to those calls, and those with other friends in faraway places who I'm blessed to have in my life. Thank you, pandemic; we're all Zoom experts now. So, turn off the TV and reach out to old friends. No excuse not to.

....lose touch with your God. Mel Brooks had a great routine in the 2000-Year-Old-Man albums recorded with straight-man Carl Reiner. When asked if he grew up believing in a higher being, Mel's ancient character proceeded to describe Phil, who was so large and strong that he could squash you like a bug. Then one day a bolt of lightning came down and struck Phil dead where he stood. To which Mel and his caveman friends exclaimed, "There's something bigger than Phil!" I've been fortunate enough to see the power of God in my life. You read about one instance in this book. I'm sure you have your own.

....fail to make a solid financial plan for your working life and retirement. So why do you think I'm still working? 'nuff said.

....cause yourself to be unhappy. A surprisingly common regret of the dying from the Susan Steiner list. What surprised me was that so many did not realize happiness is a choice. Stuck in old patterns and habits, the comfort of familiarity, fear of change, pretending to be content. They longed to "laugh properly and have silliness in their life again." One of my proudest moments lately was to go two-for-three with my grandnieces and nephew in the ever challenging, get-them-to-laugh-so-hard-they-squirt-root-beer-out-of-their-noses. Whereupon I advised Papa Joe, "You might want to hose down that room." Wife Cindy has always said she has three boys, Kyle, Corey, and me. I hope to never to lose that. Reminds me of my dad. Laugh every day from your ankles or get someone else to do so. Roman poet Horace said, "Mix a little foolishness with your prudence; it's good to be silly at the right moment."

....be afraid to take a chance. One of the hardest decisions I made in my life was to move my family to Singapore. If not for Cindy, I might not have had the guts to go. Today I look back on that experience as not only life-changing for me, but life-forming for our sons. Try to put a price tag on that.

....abandon your best life. Young or old, get out there. Have a hobby. Travel, hike, cook, read, dance. Say something obnoxious to a friend, and be creative with it (if the humor isn't appreciated, find another friend). Adopt a dog (but don't let him poop on my driveway without picking it up—I'm still looking for you), play a game with your kids or grandkids, roll bocce balls on a beach (my personal favorite). Make new friends. Experience something new (or something old). Go to museums (but don't bore me with the details), walk through a park (daytime in most locales), stay healthy. One of these days you'll look in a mirror and wonder who the geezer is staring back at you. Be proud of that person. You've earned it.

....sweat the small stuff. It's all small stuff, and you're a bright enough humanoid to recognize that by now. After all, you showed the intellectual prowess to buy this book, and now you've read it. Ok, maybe that wasn't the best example, but you get the idea.

....forget to recommend this book to others. (While we have a train of thought going, this one is for me. See 'solid financial plan' above.)

That's it. Hope you find it helpful. If not, join a support group.

Chapter Eleven

> → Life Lessons 101C:
> Short Shorts and Strange Things

This is a list of little things that have been noticed, some of them decades ago, that I cannot get out of my brain. If they would just leave, perhaps I'd remember something important for a change. In no particular order....

Another Answer to "Why Would You Live in North Dakota?"
Because I was born there, my parents were there and they gave me food.

Favorite Bumper sticker
On a TR7 in Juneau, Alaska. "Jesus is Coming and Boy is He Peeved" (Actually a different last word. Choose your own...)

Favorite Movie Line
"Shi..er was full." (Cousin Eddie on Christmas Vacation, an annual must-watch in our family.)

Favorite Country Song Title
"If I'd shot her when I wanted to, I'd be out by now" (Cindy doesn't care for this one much.)

Weirdest Christmas Party Grand Prize
At a local bar, benefiting Toys for Tots. The one and only raffle drawing was for a basket of adult sex toys from Adam & Eve.

(One of many) Favorite Responses From a Child
Kyle, age 16, when asked whatever happened to his career goal to be either a garbage man or an airplane driver. "I turned seven."

Favorite Thing Said by David Feherty
Pretty much anything.

Favorite Distance Measurement
"A Mile Down The Road And A Half" (North Dakota centric, on a sign made for me by my daughter-in-law shortly after she heard the line. Thank you, Leigh, for your creativity and thoughtfulness. It will always be in my office.)

Favorite North Dakota Joke
A visitor stops into a remote café, and asks the owner "Do you have any Norwegian Jews up here?" Owner, speaking in a thick North Dakotan German brogue: "No, but we got tomato chooz and apple chooz."

Favorite Olé and Lena Joke
Olé comes home from work dejected, and let's Lena know he has been fired. Lena: "What happened?" Olé: "I got my

pecker caught in the pickle packer." Lena: "What happened to the pickle packer?" Olé: "She got fired too." (This one might not make the cut.)

Two Favorite Sniglets (words that don't exist but should be in the dictionary):

Cussellection: The uncanny ability of a two-year-old to select as his/her latest vocabulary addition the only cuss word you have uttered for a year. (Won 50 bucks sending this one into a radio station requesting sniglets.)

Remeat: Your wife's tendency to cook for dinner the very same entree you had for lunch. (Won another $50 on this one, with a secondary definition for good measure that will not be repeated here.)

Favorite Golf Line
"I've played this game for 63 years and I haven't enjoyed a minute of it." (Credit to Dr. Fred, Cindy's last stepfather.)

Second Favorite Fiancée Line
"Now both knees can match." (as I was writhing in pain with my second knee injury. First favorite line is in the Meeting Cindy section of Chapter Three.)

Got My Attention Line By The Wife
Upon noticing an empty wine glass, I playfully asked "How can I make you happy?" Her response: "Take me to Bali." Didn't see that coming.

J012-8000-6757-1516
My driver's license number in both North Dakota (1970's) and Missouri (1980's). Get. Out. Of. My. Head.

Not So Lucky Seven
Corey in 5th grade, just before move to Singapore, throwing him 'divers' with the baseball in the backyard, just out of reach so he had to dive to make the catch. Mom calls out that it's time for dinner. He wants ten more throws. On number seven he breaks his collar bone. Seven years later in his senior year in Singapore, playing his last football game, seven minutes left, wearing number seven, he breaks the same collar bone.

Favorite Flying Punch Line
By comedian Ron White, seated next to a nervous flyer on a plane with one engine out, in response to the question, "How... how... how far do you think this plane can fly with one engine?" Ron's response: "All the way to the scene of the crash. Which is handy because that's where we're headed right now. I'll bet we beat the paramedics by 20 minutes."

Favorite Surgery Line
"I left my appendix in Council Bluffs." (There's a song in there somewhere. I actually did leave it there, but I won't bore you with the details of that or any of the other six eclectic surgeries in my life. You're welcome.)

Favorite Forwarded Email Joke
When I was young I decided I wanted to be a doctor, so I took the entrance exam to go to Medical School. One of the

questions asked was to rearrange the letters PNEIS into the name of an important human body part which is most useful when erect. Those who answered SPINE are doctors today. The rest of us are sending jokes via email.

Favorite Gravestone Epitaph
I Told You I Was Sick

Favorite Cowboy Joke
A cowboy appeared before St. Peter at the Pearly Gates.
"Have you ever done anything of particular merit?" St. Peter asked.
"Well, I can think of one thing," the cowboy offered. "On a trip to the Black Hills out in South Dakota, I came upon a gang of bikers who were threatening a young woman. I directed them to leave her alone, but they wouldn't listen. So, I approached the largest and most tattooed biker and smacked him in the face, kicked his bike over, ripped out his nose ring, and threw it on the ground. I yelled, "Now, back off or I'll kick the crap out of all of you!"
St. Peter was impressed. "When did this happen?"
"Couple of minutes ago."

Favorite Old Golfer's Joke
A couple of old guys were golfing when one mentioned that he was going to go to Dr. Steinberg for a new set of dentures the next morning.
His elderly buddy remarked that he, too, had gone to the very same dentist two years before.
"Is that so?" asked the first old guy. "Did he do a good job?"

The second oldster replied, "Well, I was on the golf course yesterday when a guy on the next fairway hooked a shot. The ball must have been going at least 180 mph when it slammed me right in the groin."

The first old guy was confused and asked, "What the hell does that have to do with your dentures?"

"It was the first time in two years my teeth didn't hurt."

Favorite Thinking Man's Joke
What does an insomniac, agnostic, dyslectic do? Lays awake at night wondering if there is a Dog.

Favorite Speeding Line
A Florida senior citizen drove his brand-new Corvette convertible out of the dealership. Taking off down the road, he pushed it to 80 mph, enjoying the wind blowing through what little hair he had left.

"Amazing," he thought as he flew down I-95, pushing the pedal even more.

Looking in his rear-view mirror, he saw a Florida state Trooper, blue lights flashing and siren blaring. He floored it to 100 mph, then 110, then 120. Suddenly he thought, "What am I doing? I'm too old for this!" and pulled over to await the trooper's arrival.

Pulling in behind him, the trooper got out of his vehicle and walked up to the Corvette. He looked at his watch, then said, "Sir, my shift ends in 30 minutes. Today is Friday. If you can give me a new reason for speeding—a reason I've never before heard—I'll let you go."

The old gentleman paused then said, "Three years ago, my wife ran off with a Florida state Trooper. I thought you were bringing her back."

"Have a good day, Sir," replied the trooper.

Favorite Bar Joke

A man walks into a bar and notices another old gentleman at the end of the bar with a rat playing a miniature piano and a frog singing along to the melody. He approaches the old man and says, "That's really impressive, how much do you want for the singing frog?"

When told he was not for sale, the man offered $1,000. Again, not for sale was the reply. "Ok, you drive a hard bargain, I'll give you $5,000 for that frog." This time the old man relented and sold him the frog.

The bartender expressed surprise to the old man that he would sell a singing frog for any price. The reply: "Oh, I have a yard full of frogs. But a ventriloquist rat that can play the piano, now that's rare."

Favorite Golf Line, Part 2

From friend and business partner Bob, "Swing easy and live with the extra distance."

Favorite Brother's T-Shirt

I Love My Dog And About Three Other People.

Favorite Response to Not Having Chest Hair

"Hair doesn't grow in steel."

(Not so) Favorite Brother Al's Chest Hair Response

"It doesn't grow on Jello either."

Best Roadside Christmas Greeting by Sunset Beach Police Department
"Cousin Eddie Says, Twitter's Full. Put Your Phone Down."

Least Favorite Speeding Ticket
Wake Forest, NC just after repatriation, hurrying to donate blood and pulled over. (No sympathy for my explanation, as apparently, the police officer DID NOT speed to make her own blood donation earlier in the day). At the blood center, most of the recent travels abroad were ok'd for donation, until the safari in Hoedspruit, South Africa came up. Denied for donation and left with a speeding ticket to pay. Welcome home.

Favorite Floating Markets
Thailand. There are many, one on the Chao Phraya River that weaves through Bangkok and allows for people to travel and sell their goods. Today the markets are also a tourist destination, and access by a long boat is great fun. Long boats are propelled by secondhand car or truck engines with extensions on the driveshaft to a propeller. A V-8 on a stick.

Favorite Floating Villages
Cambodia. Siem Reap has a number of them, of which Kampong Phluk is one we visited. In the rainy season the adjoining lake grows immensely, so homes, businesses, school and even a church (all built on 55-gallon drums) follow the water out and back. As we floated by, a tv show was being viewed by friends in a small hut. Power was

provided by 12-volt car batteries, which could be recharged at the business next door.

Favorite Street Markets
Toss-up here. Patpong Night Market in Bangkok was the first I visited so I have a soft spot. Set up and taken down on a daily basis, it is jammed with vendors selling clothing, watches, knick-knacks, etc. Universal language is the calculator, used to negotiate prices. After I came to a price on a small laser pointer, I then asked the vendor for a price on 90 of them, intended for my network of trainers. Needless to say, I made a friend that night.
And then there is Snake Alley in Taipei. It's what it sounds like. Open markets for snakes, turtles, seafood, all in various stages of 'preparation' for sale with some 'performances' since regulated away. And in the midst of the market is a fabulous seafood restaurant complete with chandeliers and Waterford crystal. Now that's eclectic.

Favorite Place to Create a Shameless Plug
Right here. I invented and developed along with good friend Bob from Pinehurst a memory foam back support with strap to attach to any chair, unique with a water-resistant cover and therapy pocket that houses a reusable cold/hot gel pack that we also sell. Provides therapy and has been used for comfort on just about anything you can sit on, from beach chairs (the beginnings of the product) to planes, trains and automobiles along with home, office, wherever. Called the B-Rite Back, it deserves a full section in this work, but I'll settle for you just surfing over to www.b-riteback.com to see for yourself and buy one. Enter

MYBRB20 in the coupon code field for a 20% discount. You're welcome.

OK, Another Shameless Plug
After you've bought your back support and are comfortably icing or heating your sore lumbar, you'll need something to Google. Enter www.justrodbooks.com, where you can spend about two minutes you'll never get back learning about my other works. I especially recommend one that weaves the concept of "Don't Do That" into a speaking engagement for which I will happily charge. It's a Do That, not a Don't Do That.

And Finally, Favorite Next Topics for a Sequel
The list is growing, but at the top of it is the wedding celebration we were attending while this book was in final edit stages. Son two Corey married the love of his life, Jeannie in Chicago. She is fantastic, they are incredibly happy and I'll do them more justice in another work.

→ Bookend

I began this book with a very brief history of my grandparent's emigration from Russia to homestead in North Dakota, after 100 years of peaceful farming by the German population there.

Sadly today, another 100 years later, the same plight faces the people of Ukraine. My grandfather listed Bobrowikist, Russia as his last place of residence upon arrival at Ellis Island. The town is today's Bobrovyi Kut, in southern Ukraine and about 275 miles due west of the seaport city of Mariupol. As of this writing the town is occupied by Russian troops.

I urge you to enter this url into your browser when you have 30 minutes to spare. It chronicles the emigrant's struggle from the last century, and is a poignant reminder of how we 'advanced' beings can still find ways to inflict misery upon each another. But more importantly, it illustrates the strength of the human spirit.

God bless my people.

https://youtu.be/1TyXHaNWaaM

→ Epilogue of Gratitude

This work has been both a joy to write and therapeutic for the soul. I think we get busy with day to day to the point that we lose track of the sum total of the entertaining episodes in our lives. I mentioned early in this work that I was always disappointed in not having the opportunity to see my maternal grandfather's perspective on the family move from Russia to the Unites States. Mom wrote a high school paper on the topic, and sadly did not retain it. So perhaps a grandchild or two will find a bit of entertainment and insight from the words shared here.

I was blessed with two wonderful parents. They came from a time that parents didn't necessarily say the words "I love you", but showed it every day with their actions. They taught by example; they worked hard, laughed from the ankles, worshiped their God, did the right thing and helped others without expectation. Dad has been gone for over fifty years as of this writing and Mom for twelve. Neither passing seems nearly that long ago. Such is their lasting impact.

My one brother would happily tell you that I was blessed with him. In point of fact I idolized him growing up and continue to be impressed by that disgustingly natural golf swing, his decisiveness, success at business and cutting sense of humor that I happily adopted. His wife

Kathy has been a rock with him for going on a half century now. The two of them are gourmet cooks. Al's "locally famous French Onion Soup" and Kathy's green chili breakfast burritos are life-changing, to name just two of their many transcendent delectables.

I have been blessed with a wonderful wife of now 40 years. I always say (much to her chagrin) that "she's blessed" and for decades reminded her that we had a 40-year contract. In May, 2021—just over a year ago—she entered her option year, critical to the contract extension. This year we celebrated that all important 40th, but rather than a contract extension, I gave her a franchise tag.[2]

In point of fact her strength, cutting sense of humor, skills as the quintessential boy-mom, independence and wanderlust that pushed me to see the world with her have been my foundation.

Cindy blessed me with two terrific boys, who were a joy to raise and have turned into fine young men whom I've seen put themselves in harm's way to do the right thing. Kyle and Corey grew up strong and to this day at ages 37 and 35 continue to play competitive rugby, proof positive that toughness skips a generation. They are smart, seem to have found their paths in life, and both made terrific choices in the women with whom they will share their lives. Grandson Locke and Granddaughter Carter are a joy and we hope to be blessed with others. What more could a parent ask for?

---

[2] "A franchise tag is a designation a team may apply to a player scheduled to become an unrestricted free agent. The tag binds the player to the team for one year if certain conditions are met."
—Wikipedia   That's footnote number 2. Positively academic!

As a family we were blessed for the opportunity to see the world. Beyond my work travels, how can you not appreciate watching your sons bungee jump in New Zealand, play baseball in four different countries, softball in three more and football in another? Or have a private boat take you around Hong Kong and to Llama Island for a memorable meal? Or seeing sights and enjoying magnificent cuisine in Thailand, China, Viet Nam, Cambodia, London and Paris, to name a few? Or sail fish in Malaysia or take a safari in South Africa? Or play golf in exotic places you never could imagine, with kangaroos hopping alongside your golf cart in Australia, to name one. The thirtieth country capital I visited for the first time was my own.

From Linton and Bismarck, North Dakota, and Mount Vernon Ohio, to Denver to St. Louis to Singapore to Wake Forest to Sunset Beach, North Carolina, the good Lord seems to have placed us in the right place for each stage of our lives, the occasional lack of personal planning notwithstanding. We have met and enjoyed countless interesting and wonderful people from all walks of life. I look forward to the next (hopefully somewhat eclectic) chapter and remain thankful for all that I have.

One difficult part of this work is to stop. Every story recollected kept bringing to mind another. And another. Some listed above, others still floating in the recesses of my brain. I'll save those for another day.

Seems that we have done a few things just right. But there's still time to fix that...